PSYCHIC

PLAIN & SIMPLE

PSYCHIC ABILITY

PLAIN & SIMPLE

UNLOCK YOUR INTUITION AND DISCOVER THE POWER OF PERCEPTION

ANN CAULFIELD

THE ONLY BOOK YOU'LL EVER NEED

HAMPTON ROADS

Cover design by Jim Warner
Cover art © Seregy7 / bigstock
Interior design by Kathryn Sky-Peck

Hampton Roads Publishing Company, Inc.
Charlottesville, VA 22906
Distributed by Red Wheel/Weiser, LLC
www.redwheelweiser.com
Sign up for our newsletter and special offers by going to
www.redwheelweiser.com/newsletter

ISBN: 978-1-57174-772-3
Library of Congress Control Number: 2017942304
Printed in the Unites States of America
IBI
10 9 8 7 6 5 4 3 2 1

Contents

This book is dedicated to my husband Peter,

who has always been there for me

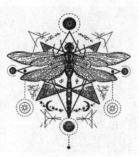

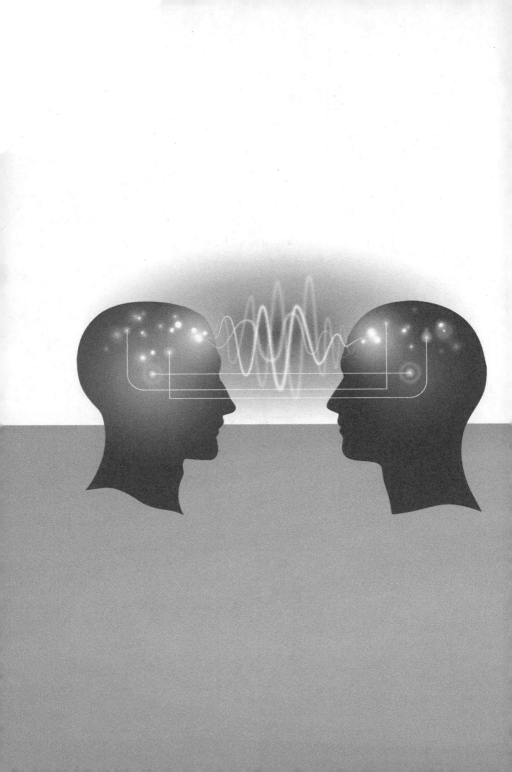

What Is
Psychic
Ability?

To be intuitive is to be psychic; therefore, everyone is psychic to some degree. Our intuition is a natural energy that is present from birth; it ranges from a normal, light awareness to the heavy, dense ectoplasm used by physical mediums. The abilities of the majority of people who develop their psychic faculties are somewhere in the middle. If you had an "imaginary" friend as a child or have ever had a hunch, a knowing, or a premonition, then you have the ability to develop your psychic faculties to a higher degree. The expansion of your psychic senses can help you to achieve far more from your life than you do now. It will also help you to understand others and to get on with them better.

As you develop and nurture your psychic faculties, it is the little things that matter. In this book, I will draw your attention to some that you should be aware of, for example, using your sense of touch (being conscious of a light pressure on your head, ears, or throat); taking notice of that sudden lurch in your stomach, or a rapid change in mood; and recognizing a psychic flash of light across a page or the flicker of color around any living thing.

Telepathy, known as extrasensory perception (ESP), is another type of psychic aptitude. Developing any of these abilities can lead you along a very exciting pathway of exploration, stimulating senses that members of the general populace no longer use fully.

I will teach you the following forms of development, known as "emotional mediumship":

- How to open and develop your psychic centers (chakras)

- How to reveal the history of an object by holding it (psychometry)

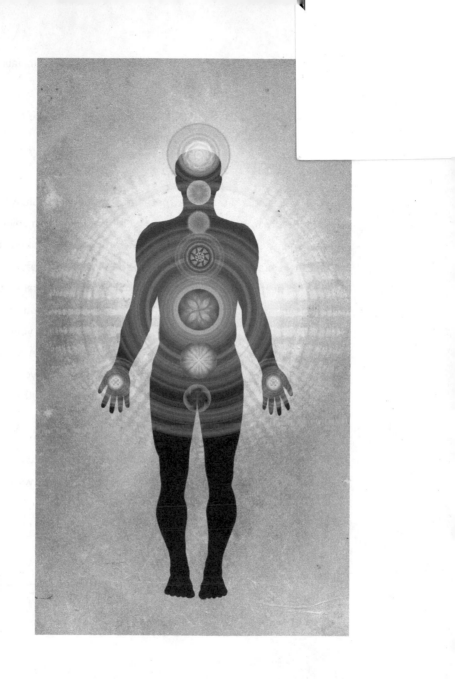

- How to read the past and present of the human aura (auric reading), a higher level of mediumship

- How to read the higher vibrations of someone's aura through a flower (flower clairsentience)

- How to perform astral travel

If you find that these aspects of emotional mediumship come easily to you, then you may well have positive, mediumistic energy, in which case you may wish to work on a far higher spiritual vibration. Do you believe that our souls live on after our physical death? If you do, then you can take the all-important step of communicating with the dimension of spirit. When you reach this level, there is no turning back, as you will be offering yourself up to the service of spirit. If you develop your psychic centers to this degree, the gift will remain with you for the rest of your life, but it will always have to be used for the well-being of others as well as for yourself.

Commitment along this pathway must be considered carefully. If you decide to continue, however, it will probably be the most rewarding and uplifting spiritual revelation that you will ever encounter.

You will also discover mental mediumship in the form of:

- Clairvoyance (seeing spirit)

- Clairaudience (hearing spirit)

- Clairsentience (feeling spirit)

I will show you how to recognize and describe spirits, how to listen to what they tell you, and how to pick up information from them about a person's past, present, and future,

I will also show you the different methods of closing your centers and cleansing your aura at the end of a session, to protect you and ground you once more in the physical world.

Are you ready to meet the challenge of this incredible journey? If so, read on.

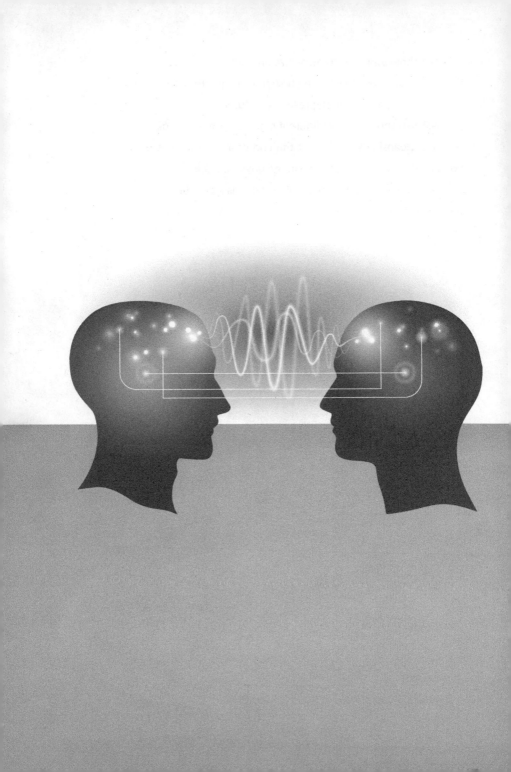

Telepathy
(ESP)

1

Apart from our five senses—taste, touch, smell, sight, and hearing—there is one other sense that we all have in common, but it is often ignored or not developed to its full potential. It is our intuition, which is a natural energy that is present in all of us from birth. The strength of our intuition denotes the strength of our psychic ability.

Thousands of years ago, before the invention of language, we used our psychic senses to survive, by sensing danger, for example, or by sensing the presence of prey when we hunted for food. Today, however, advancements in technology have made it unnecessary for us to use our psychic faculties in this way. Despite these improvements in our modern-day lives, as we human beings strive to better ourselves on a material level, we sometimes feel empty and unfulfilled. Now more than ever, people are searching for the meaning of life. Some people investigate different religions, while others—the younger generation in particular—are turning to alternative means for insight and spiritual growth, openly studying mediumship and the development of the psychic faculty on a personal and scientific level. In fact, there are many reports that prior knowledge of events— intuition—has now been scientifically proven.

When I ask people if they think they are psychic, the answer is often an emphatic "no." When I then ask them if they have ever thought about someone, only to have that person contact them within a short space of time, almost all of them agree that they have experienced this. Further probing reveals that they have often said the same thing at the same time as someone they are with. Most of them say they have sometimes had premonitions about a distant friend or relative who was ill, and everyone has reported feeling a churning in the stomach before bad news. Many of them agree that there have been times when they've had a hunch about something, which they didn't follow through on, only to discover that their hunch was correct all along. These are all instances of telepathy, but they are such everyday occurrences in our lives that they are often classed as coincidences.

Zenner Cards

The American parapsychologist Joseph Banks Rhine used playing cards to test the telepathic reactions in his subjects. As there were fifty-two cards in a pack, the tests took such a long time to conduct that Rhine began searching for a quicker method of detecting extrasensory perception (ESP). His colleague Karl Zenner was an expert in the psychology of perception, and Rhine persuaded him to design a set of five cards, each with an unambiguous design on it. Zenner produced a set of psi-cards that contained a circle, a wavy line, a cross, a square, and a star. These cards were used as a simple tool for assessing extrasensory perception, and

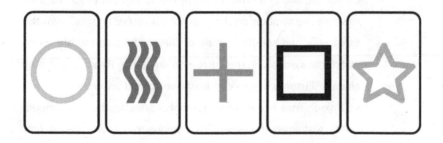

they are still in use today. If you wish to test how telepathic you are, I recommend that you try using Zenner cards. They can be bought from any good New Age retailer, or you can easily make up your own set. Each deck of twenty-five cards consists of five sets of five cards for each basic symbol, with the numbers 1 to 25 on the backs.

Using Zenner Cards to Test Your Powers of ESP

Here's the way to assess your extrasensory perception: Take a pad and pen and write down the numbers 1 to 25. Put the pen and writing pad down next to you, and then sit quietly for a few minutes. When you feel ready, shuffle your deck of Zenner cards and lay them facedown on the table. Take the first card from the deck, keeping it facedown, and place it in front of you. Relax as much as possible; let your mind be still. Don't think about what the card is. Wait for a moment until an image of a symbol forms in your mind. If you cannot see an image but you have a strong feeling about what the card is, make a note of this first image next to the number 1 on your pad. Now do the same for all the other cards. Be honest, and don't turn over any of the cards until you've tried to sense the symbols on them all. When you've finished, turn the cards over and see how many of the symbols you wrote down match the symbols on the corresponding cards. Random guessing alone will usually produce at least five correct answers.

If you sense five or more symbols correctly, then you should try the test again, this time with someone to help you. Your helper should shuffle the cards, then take the first one from the deck and hold it up in front of him or her with the back toward you (if you are familiar with which symbols are on which cards, ask your helper to cover the back of the card so you can't see the number). Then write down on your pad what you think the symbol is. Your helper should write down the symbol next to the corresponding number on his or her own pad. If you match ten or more symbols and cards, then you have exceptional powers of ESP.

Determining Your Mediumistic Ability with Zenner Cards

If you have been successful with the basic test and you want to see if you have mediumistic ability, both you and your helper should sit quietly and try to clear your minds of random thoughts. It is impossible to empty the mind completely, but it is important to try to keep your thoughts still and quiet by being as relaxed as possible. For this experiment, your helper is the "sender," and you are the "receiver." The sender should shuffle the cards, then take the first one from the deck and look at the symbol. After placing the card to one side, the sender should write down the symbol and the number, and then face you, trying to hold the picture of the symbol in his or her mind. When you see an image of a symbol, or think you know what it is, you should write it down, without speaking. Repeat this process until all the cards have been used. You and the sender can then switch roles, and you can see how well you do as a sender. It is well known that mediums are receivers, picking up thoughts from other people and from spirit beings, but you may also be able to transmit energies, as does a healer.

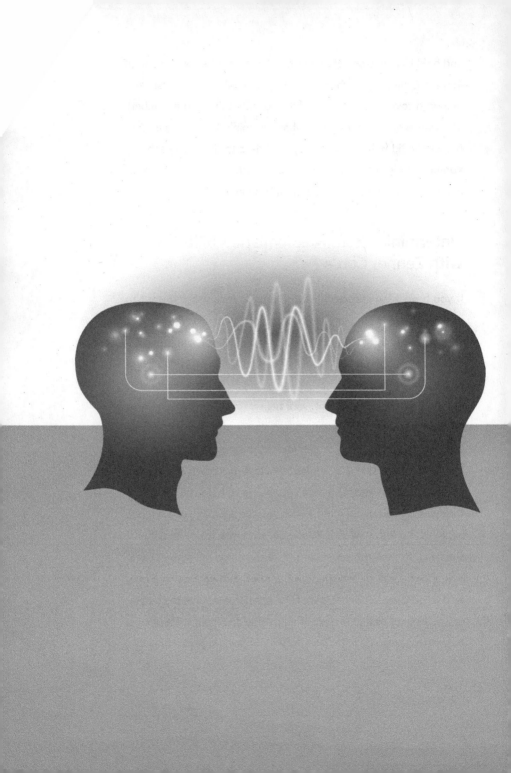

Dreams

2

Of course, you cannot say you are a medium simply from one test. You will need to repeat the experiment several times more, and also evaluate other psychic factors to see whether you can develop your ability further. Many people claim that they don't dream, but we all do. Some people simply cannot remember their dreams. The problem with dreams is that unless you write them down as soon as you wake up, they quickly fade. Most of our dreaming, even prophetic dreaming, is in the form of symbolism: mixed-up versions of events and information that we've absorbed during our waking hours. Did you know that some people dream only in black and white, while others dream in color?

On occasion, our dreams are vivid, detailed, and prophetic; these are the dreams that you should take special note of. It's not that these types of dreams are easy to forget, but if you get into the habit of writing them down, you will have a written record to refer to at a later date. Here is an example of a vivid dream that I had a few years ago, which remains as clear to me today as it was when I woke up from it.

> I was standing in a small, bare room facing the door, which was open a little. The room was dark, but a yellow gleam from the hall light penetrated the dimness. I could clearly hear the loud thumps of footsteps coming up the hall, and I felt terrified of what I thought was a monster looking for me. At the same time, I was aware of a figure dressed in robes, standing to my left in the corner. The footsteps stopped, and the door swung open. It revealed a giant of a man who had to duck to get through the doorway. When he lifted his head, I saw the contorted features of my husband, Peter.

He walked toward me with his arms outstretched . . . and
at this point I woke up.

I lay there trying to analyze the dream, sure that something
unpleasant was about to happen, and sure that it involved Peter.
I realized that it was going to be scary because of the fear I had
felt and because of the painful expression I had seen on Peter's
face. Whatever it was involved me, too, because he was walking
toward me with his arms outstretched. I thought the figure in the
corner was a guide.

I told Peter about the dream, and we were both wary because
I've had prophetic dreams before, and although I didn't know
what was going to happen, we both knew we had to be prepared

for the worst. We had sold our house and were moving abroad, and we wondered if we were being warned not to go. At that stage, we felt we couldn't do much about it and had to wait and see what happened.

A few days later, while I continued to pack up boxes, Peter took our dog, Rhea, for a long walk through the forest. When he returned, he told me that on the way back he had seen a dog running loose without its owner. Peter knew the dog lived in a house he had already passed. He called the dog over, returned to the house, and delivered the dog safely. Then he once again started out on his journey home.

While he was telling me this story, he was rubbing his chest, so I asked him if he was in pain. He said he had felt several instances of pain while he was out and thought it was indigestion. Knowing he hadn't eaten anything since breakfast, I thought this was doubtful. As we spoke, he clutched his left arm and doubled over. His face was gray, and he was in agony with the pain in his chest. I realized he was having a heart attack and called an ambulance and our doctor. Both arrived within minutes. He was taken to the hospital, where the heart attack was confirmed, and he was kept there until he was well enough to come home.

This is how I analyzed my dream:

The agony I saw on Peter's face in my dream was the pain he was feeling from the heart attack. The dark room represented the dark time we both experienced, not knowing whether he would come through it or not. I saw him as a giant, and to me this indicated how big and serious the heart attack could be, but the light from the hallway told me he had a chance of living through it. His outstretched arms represented him turning toward me for help. The figure in the corner of the room did turn out to be a guide—someone watching over him. The dream didn't tell me that Peter's pain would be caused by a heart attack, but because I always take note of my dreams, I have learned to assess any symbolism I see.

In this way, I've gradually learned to judge each individual part of a dream until it feels right. With this dream I didn't know exactly what was going to happen, but I did know that it was bad and that it would be connected more with Peter than with me. For these reasons, I now always keep notepaper and a pen by the bed so that I can write down anything significant I dream about.

The Beckoning Grave

British author J. B. Priestley received a letter containing the following information in response to his appeal for experiences in which the conventional idea of "time" was upset.

A little girl dreamed she was walking up the path of an old church graveyard with her long, wet hair clinging to her. Around her were several horses aimlessly walking around. She found that she was drawn to one particular grave, but when she reached it she had a horrifying sensation of falling. At this point, she woke up feeling depressed. For as far back as she could remember, she'd had the same dream over and over again, which never varied in any way. But one day she had an experience that chased the dream away forever.

APRIL 29,
1934

At the age of twelve, while she was on vacation, she was caught in a thunderstorm on her way to her relatives' home. Suddenly, she came upon the church of her dream, exact in every detail. In fact, she found that she was living the dream. Her long, wet hair clung to her, some ponies were wandering around the area, and a certain grave drew her toward it. When she got to the grave, she saw the death date on the headstone: "April 29th 1934." That date was her birthday. After seeing this, she never had the dream again.

The most obvious meaning of this dream is that the girl was having a deja vu experience. Or perhaps the person who died was reincarnated into the young girl at the time of her birth. This is speculation, of course, but it is well known that J. B. Priestley was very interested in psychic phenomena and theories of the way that time and reincarnation played themselves out.

Lincoln's Death Dream

Another example of a prophetic dream was reported by the great American president Abraham Lincoln, who foresaw his own death. In the dream, he saw himself standing at the foot of a coffin in the White House. A soldier was standing nearby, and Lincoln asked him who had died. The soldier told him that it was the president, and that an assassin had killed him.

Most of us now know, of course, that an assassin killed Lincoln while he was at the theater one night.

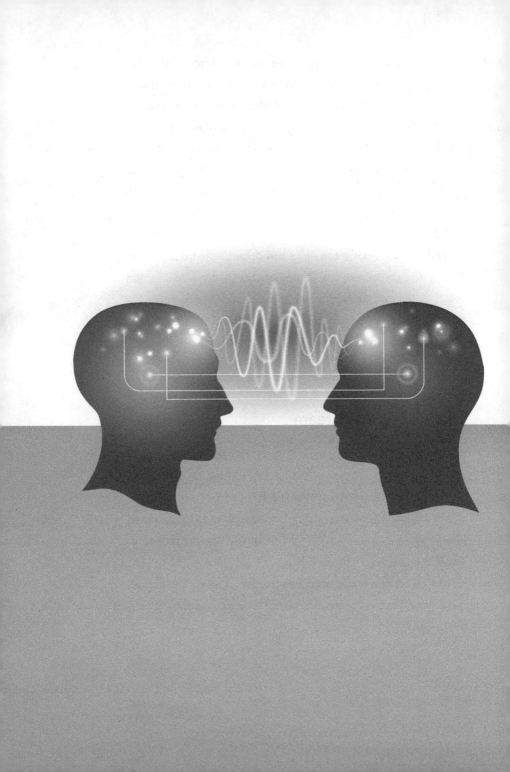

Psychic Centers (Chakras)

3

In this chapter, I will show you what you can achieve by developing and working with the first four chakras—the "emotional" chakras. Information about the development of the other three chakras (the "mental" chakras) can be found in Chapter 13, where the subject of mediumship is covered. Developing your chakras, which I also call psychic centers, will help you to gain the most from your chosen pathway.

A brief study of any religion will reveal that human beings are more than just physical forms. Since your spirit is a reality, the level of your spiritual development will direct your physical life, even though you may not be consciously aware of this. Each

human being is a trinity; the physical, psychic, and spiritual bodies interpenetrate one another. Our bodies contain many of these psychic centers, but the major chakras used for psychic work lie close to important glands and nerve endings. Your psychic and physical health will be affected by the activity of these centers and their influence on the nerves and glands adjacent to them.

Each center, or chakra, has its own special function, and most people have one chakra that is more active than the others. However, if you wish to develop your psychic faculties, it is important that you develop each center to the best of your ability. Although in mediumship one center in particular will be used, all of the psychic centers rely on one another to work well together.

Psychic Center Number One

There are seven main centers used for psychic development: four emotional centers and three mental centers. The emotional chakras are centers of "feeling." The first one is situated at the base of the spine. This area is where all your spiritual energy is stored, and you must learn how to draw this energy up and through each center, as they all depend on this base chakra in some way. When you have correctly activated this energy with your mind, you should feel a physical sensation creeping through the lower part of your body. When working with this center, close your eyes for a moment and focus on a mental picture of this area of your body, and you may see a misty or smoky substance swirling around. This substance may be shot with small darting lights, or even small flashes of red.

Psychic Center Number Two

The second center is the largest of all the chakras. Located in the middle of the abdomen, this center is extremely sensitive to emotional influences. In fact, all negative emotion is felt through this center. It is the area that mediums use the most, especially when performing psychometry and when dealing with physical phenomena. Through this center you feel a lurch, a premonition, or any kind of shock or disturbance. This chakra is also dependent on feelings.

Psychic Center Number Three

The third emotional center is in the area of the diaphragm. Although it works in a similar way to the second center, the frequency of the energy from this center is faster. It acts as a kind of filter for the sensations, separating the good from the bad and giving a more positive interpretation of events than the second center, although still through the medium of feeling. It is also through this center that astral travel occurs.

Psychic Center Number Four

Center number four is in the region of the heart, and its energy is much finer than that of the first three centers, although it still works on the emotional level. The fourth center is the doorway to the mental centers, even though it is an emotional center. It is the area of compassion and understanding. A healer, an energy worker who can pick up and actually feel physical sensations from a patient, uses this center. The pain and anxiety that the healer feels while working on a patient can be very real. The healer may even be aware of the presence of spirit, but this center will not give true details of what is going on with a patient unless used in conjunction with the mental centers, which are described next.

Psychic Center Number Five

The fifth center is in the region of the throat and is the first of the mental centers. This is the seat of clairaudience, through which one can hear the voice of spirit. Some mediums hear a voice that they describe as coming from their throats. Others, like me, hear the voice of spirit on one side of the head or the other, close to the region of the ear. A message that comes in this way is so clear and straightforward that the medium can be quite confident when passing it on to the person for whom it is meant.

This center works with the second and fourth centers when a medium is passing messages while in a trance. Developed properly, it is the clearest and most reliable area of information out of all the psychic centers. In fact, investigators have discovered that this area can operate on a non-mediumistic level. They have found that painters, writers, and creative artists of all kinds make full use of their throat centers for their art, although they are probably unaware that they are doing so.

Psychic Center Number Six

The best-known psychic center is number six, the clairvoyant, or third eye. This is the seat of genuine clairvoyance. The clairaudient and clairvoyant centers work together in this center on a faster frequency than each one works individually, although one  of these two will dominate, depending on the medium. Because of the speed with which they work, the information provided can sometimes be too fast to hear or see clearly, but if you mentally ask spirit to repeat it, this will be done until you are sure of the message. These two centers are mutually supportive, and you can move from one to the other easily.

Much of what passes for clairvoyance—especially from the undeveloped practitioner—is simply imagery that a person stirs up on an emotional level. However, once you have developed the sixth psychic center properly, you will never mistake your experiences of either clairvoyance or clairaudience for imagination or wishful thinking. The picture a medium receives through this center appears in three-dimensional form, with each mark, hair, or blemish in view. In addition, the medium can "zoom in" on the image to add clarity or examine only one part. Once you see such a picture, and the clarity of light surrounding it, it remains with you. Simple imagery, in contrast, is similar to memory in that it is flat and lacks that special light and clarity. Subjective clairvoyance and clairaudience always enter the head on opposite sides. Once clairvoyance enters your mind, it fills it in much the same way as though you were recalling a scene that you recently saw on the television.

Psychic Center Number Seven

The crown is the seventh and last center used for psychic work. Like center number one, the base chakra, it is not psychic in itself, but it provides the energy needed to stimulate psychic activity. In particular, the crown center supplies the finer spiritual energy that is required for spiritual forces to enter. As the psychic force rises through the lower centers, it awakens into activity a cosmic consciousness. It is as though one sees, hears, and understands everything at once. Because mediumship is a calling, it is dependent on the medium's willingness to work with spirit. It is at this center that the spirit of the medium, and the whole of the medium's psychic and spiritual development, blend and become one.

Closing the Psychic Centers

After psychic activity, it is important to "close" your centers and cleanse your aura, to ensure that you do not retain any unpleasant conditions. This is particularly important for the healer. One must always leave the base and crown centers open, as these are where your sources of energy are located. It is impossible to fully close off the centers, but by applying yourself mentally, you ground yourself back in the physical world again.

Always close the psychic eye (the sixth center) first. With practice, you will find your own method of closing your centers, but the following has been helpful to many mediums. Visualize each petal of a flower closing to form a tight bud. If you find that the petals want to close all together, this procedure is too slow for you. Either let the petals fold rapidly or use a different method. Visualizing a door slamming shut is very effective, as is "pushing" the smokelike energy back down through each center with your mind. Whichever method is right for you, use it to close each center, until all the energy is stored once again at the base of the spine. Remember—this center and the crown center remain open.

Don't worry if you forget and close all seven centers, as the ones that need to stay open will remain ajar. I knew someone who became dizzy and almost fell over when trying to close all her centers.

When this process is finished, visualize a white light above your head, and then mentally "pull" it through the whole of your body. You may feel the energy of this cleansing light running through your fingers and toes. In many ways, the closing procedure is more important than the opening procedure. This is because our centers open automatically whenever we do anything on an artistic level, such as reading, writing, painting, singing, and the like, and they also open if you are discussing or reading about the psychic field. If you get into the habit of closing your centers and cleansing your aura, you will feel more energetic and grounded in your everyday life.

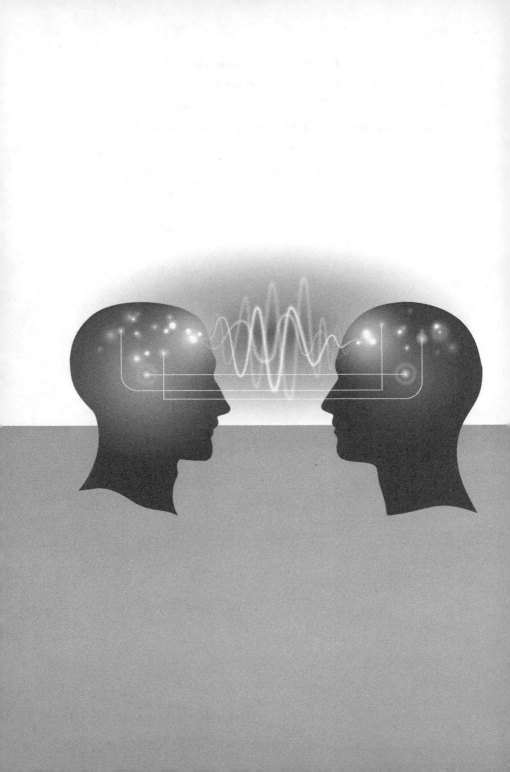

Emotional
Mediumship

4

Emotional mediumship comprises hunches, gut instinct, as well as thinking about someone and then seeing or hearing from that person minutes later. Telepathy (apart from spirit speaking), psi-cards, tarot cards, and playing cards also fall under this heading.

The chakras are an important element of mediumship. Unfortunately, negative feelings are felt through the second psychic center, which is the largest center in the body, so, because of this center's size, we are often more aware of unhappy events than of happy ones. Sudden lurches or a churning in the stomach, or feelings of bad news, for instance, are all felt in the second chakra.

The chakras, or psychic centers, lie along the spine and extend throughout the body from the back to the front. They appear as small vortices of energy, spinning at great speed. The organs they lie close to convey impressions from the inner world of spirit to physical consciousness. Therefore, the amount of psychic energy received depends on the development of all these centers.

The physical body, the home of the chakras, is surrounded by the aura, which contains the astral body and the spiritual body. In the late 1950s, Dr. W. J. Kilner and his wife published their research on a fascinating process of capturing the invisible energy field that they said radiates from every living organism.

Their evidence showed the aura to be a field of energy that is constantly moving, the inner edge of which can be seen with the physical eye. This inner band is called the "etheric body," and it surrounds two additional bands that intermingle with each other. The second band appears as smoke pouring from the body; it resembles the shimmer of a heat haze. The third band is full of color, with lights and shapes darting toward and away from the physical body. Only a clairvoyant can see these last two bands. Some mediums "read" the colors, lights, and shapes in the aura, but they are rare. I know of only one person who can do this. A friend of mine knows of another, Nina Ashby, who specializes in reading and interpreting auras.

Testing Your Powers of Mediumship

Here's one way to test how strong your powers of mediumship are or can be: Turn off your phone and make sure you won't be otherwise disturbed while performing this exercise. Wear comfortable clothes and sit in a straight-backed chair.

- Uncross your arms and legs, and close your eyes.

- Begin by taking several deep breaths and relaxing your feet.

- Tense your feet, and then relax them.

- Work your way up your body, tensing your calves, and then letting go, then tensing your thighs and your buttocks, and relaxing.

- Next, clench and unclench your hands, and then bring your elbows up to shoulder height, draw your elbows together in front of your face, contract the muscles in your arms, and lower them again.

- Tense your back by squeezing your shoulder blades together, stick out your chest, and lift your shoulders. Pay particular attention to the back of your neck, being sure that it is relaxed, but be gentle.

- Next, open your mouth and pull back your lips. Scrunch up your face and tense your forehead, then relax them.

By the time you've finished, you will be feeling calm and relaxed.

- Now, offer a small prayer to a spirit to help, guide, and protect you, and know in your heart that spirit will be with you.

- With your eyes closed, try to imagine a brilliant white light above you, shining through the top of your head, down through your body, and out through your feet.

- With your mind, try to "drag" the light several times through your body, where it will cleanse you and prepare you for work. Try to stay relaxed. You will not be able to clear all thoughts from your mind, but if you find yourself straying, bring your mind back to the task at hand and continue.

- Now focus your mind on the base of your spine. You can either imagine the chakras placed along your back, or, if it is easier, simply see a void through that part of your body.

- Visualize a glass tube rising from the base of this void and going out through the top of your head. If you concentrate on the bottom of the tube, you may see a wisp of smoke, some sudden sparks of light, or even a few red flashes.

The emotional centers will allow you to tap into only the past and present; they cannot foretell the future. However, there is much that you can achieve through using your emotional faculties, as you will see.

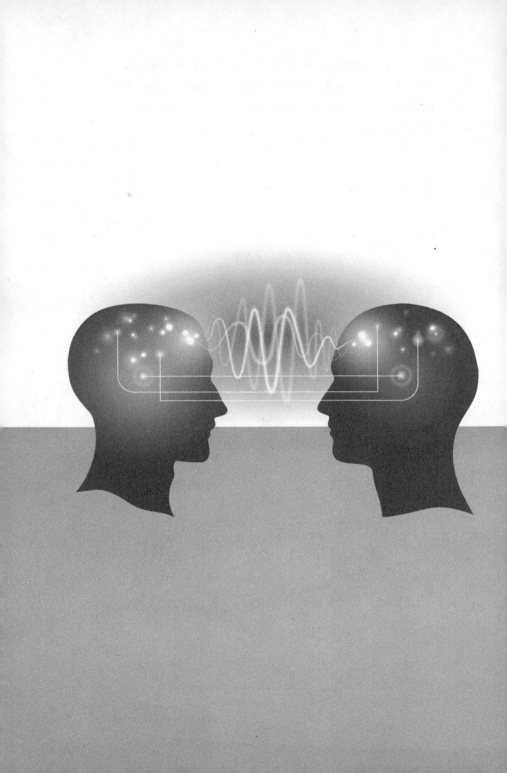

Dowsing

5

Traditionally, most dowsers divine for water, but in fact you can divine for almost anything. You will need a pair of diving rods, which you can buy from any New Age retailer or over the Internet. Just ensure that the handles are in some kind of sleeve so that the rods can swing freely.

Dowsing with Rods

Open your emotional centers (see Chapter 4), and pick up your rods. Hold the plastic sleeves without letting your fingers touch any part of the metal rods. Check that the rods move around easily, and give them a few gentle swings to get the feel of them.

Hold the rods out in front of you at a distance of about ten to twelve inches (twenty-five to thirty centimeters) from your body, with your hands about eight inches (twenty centimeters) apart. If you feel that you require more space, don't be afraid to stretch out. Beginners tend to hold the rods too close to their bodies, which can make them difficult to use. You need to be relaxed. To prevent the rods from swinging from side to side, raise and lower the ends of the rods until you feel you have control over them. (Try not to grip the handles too tightly.) You will find that it takes a little practice to hone this skill.

Next, think of the word "yes," and keep thinking of it until the dowsing rods begin to react. They may start to tremble and slowly begin to move. They usually cross, but they may part, or one rod may swing across while the other swings outward. Whatever movements the rods make are your sign for "yes," and you should be able to replicate the same action every time you think "yes."

Now think of the word "no." The rods should react differently this time. These movements are your sign for "no."

Now you are ready to ask your question. It must be a clear question that requires a simple yes-or-no answer. There's no point in asking whether you should date Pete or Alan, as dowsing can't help you answer this question. Instead, you should ask whether you should date Pete and see what answer you get. Then try the same thing for Alan.

Not only can you can use the rods to answer questions, but you can use them to look for something physical such as something that you have mislaid around the house. Take the rods and hold them out in front of you so that they are parallel to each other. Don't let them droop down, or gravity will stop them from moving freely. When you want to look for something, mentally ask your guides to show you where the lost object is, then very slowly turn in a circle and wait for the rods to move so that they cross each other. When they do so, allow them to straighten again, and then move in the direction that the rods suggested. Ask for them to cross as you get nearer to the object. Soon you will see what you are looking for.

Dowsing with a Pendulum

Dowsing can also be done with a pendulum. Pendulums are readily available for purchase from New Age retailers or over the Internet. The weight should be on a thread or chain that is around twelve inches (thirty centimeters) in length.

To dowse with a pendulum, open your psychic centers as before, and then hold the pendulum in one hand, allowing about

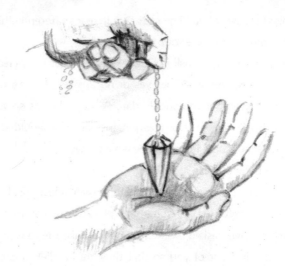

six or seven inches (fifteen or seventeen centimeters) of chain or thread for the pendulum to dangle downward. Hold the pendulum a few inches above the palm of your other hand; then think "yes" and keep thinking "yes" until the pendulum reacts.

The pendulum may move back and forth, from side to side, or in a circle. It may swing wildly or it may move only a little. Whatever movement the pendulum makes is your sign for "yes." (You can check this by trying the experiment again later.) Once you have found your "yes," repeat the process to find your sign for "no." You are now ready to use your pendulum to answer questions that require a positive or negative reply.

Dowsing Over an Illustration

One relatively easy way to dowse is over an illustration. Here's how: Ask an acquaintance to draw a rough outline of his or her house without marking which room is which. Dowse over the illustration, asking the pendulum to find a particular room in the house, such as the kitchen. The pendulum will react once you are over the part of the house that you have asked the pendulum to identify. Try to find a second type of room, and then ask for more specific information, such as the position of the refrigerator or the television.

You may even find that while you are doing these experiments, you begin to get visions of the house in your mind's eye. Check your findings with your friend by describing what you see, because the chances are that you will be right. This will be a bigger surprise to you than it will be to your friend!

If you mislay something, your pendulum will lead you to the place where you left it. Simply hold your pendulum over a design of your office, home, or car, or any other place that you wish to search. If you receive any visions while you are doing this, relax and allow them in. If you are dowsing over a sketch of a friend's house or workplace, describe anything that you see in your mind and ask your friend to give you feedback.

Dowsing Over a Map

You can also try dowsing over a map. This is a good exercise if you are thinking of moving to a different area. If you have identified two or more areas as likely places for you to move, then hold your pendulum over the map and ask, one at a time, whether that area would be the best one to move to. If you get a strong reaction from two or more areas, then the pendulum is telling you that any of them will be good for you.

Some mediums or dowsers have helped the police by dowsing over a map to help look for a murder weapon or a missing person.

Dowsing Over a Drawing

Another effective way to dowse is over a drawing. Try this with a friend. Ask a friend to think about another friend who is sick or to think about some part of his or her body that is not functioning properly. Then ask your friend to draw an image of the person in question. The drawing doesn't need to be a work of art—even a stick figure will work. Your friend just needs to concentrate on the sick person while drawing.

Now take your pendulum and start at the top of the drawing, slowly moving the pendulum from side to side, and gradually progressing down the illustration. Repeat the process a couple more times if necessary to corroborate your results. You should find that the pendulum becomes active when it reaches the part of the body that is out of balance. Alternatively, it may stick to the affected part of the body as if it is drawn to it, and it may feel as though it doesn't want to move away from the area. Discuss your findings with your friend.

While you're dowsing over the drawing, you may find yourself picking up an image of the sick person in your mind's eye. You may feel that a particular part of the body in the picture is trying to get your attention or to climb into your mind in some way. You may feel different from normal in some way, perhaps by feeling colder or warmer than usual, or you may feel a pain in your body that you somehow "know" isn't yours or a sensation of sadness or joy that belongs to someone else. Feelings of this kind are called clairsentience. You may get a distinct impression of a particular kind of ailment, or you may even begin to pick up information on when or how it started and its possible prognosis.

In addition, you may feel some vague aches and pains in your own body. If this happens, once you have finished the dowsing session, sit quietly, close off your centers, and imagine a brilliant white light suddenly being switched on above your head and flooding every part of your body. You won't catch anything from the sick person, but you may be left with some discomfort for a while unless you get rid of it by closing your centers and psychically cleansing yourself. If you find that you seem to work well in healing situations, then you could be mediumistic; if so, you would benefit from developing your mental centers too.

It is very important to close your centers after any experiment you have conducted. Close your centers as described earlier and finally cleanse with the light. This process is necessary to ground you in the physical world again.

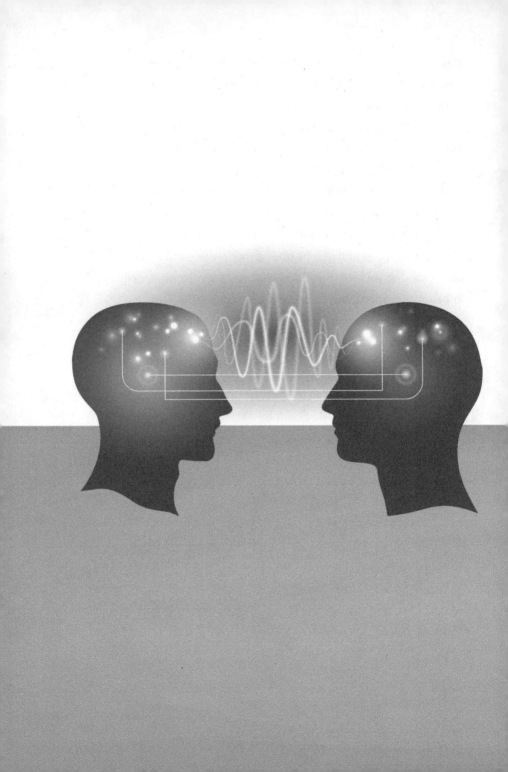

Auric, or Person-to-Person, Reading

6

A fully experienced medium can pick up your feelings through your aura upon first meeting you, even if you try hard to hide your emotions. During a reading, however, an experienced medium will always wait until those in spirit make contact before giving you genuine communication.

Nearly everyone has experienced some form of auric reading. How many times have you answered the phone to hear the voice of someone you were just thinking of? Have you ever opened the door to find the person you were thinking about standing there? How often have you been able to tell if there is something wrong with a family member or friend, just by looking at his or her face or hearing his or her voice? You probably didn't know what was wrong, only that you could feel it. This is because you have tapped into that person's aura with your own. You can connect with the aura of any person, no matter how far away he or she is. It doesn't matter if the person is in the room with you or on the other side of the world; you can still make that link.

Reading the Aura of a Friend

Try reading the aura of a friend. Here's how.

- Ask your friend to relax and sit comfortably.

- You sit opposite, preferably in a straight-backed chair. If you sit in an armchair, you may become so relaxed that it will be too much effort for you to work.

- Explain to your friend that you must spend a few minutes opening your centers.

- Then close your eyes, take several deep breaths, and relax, beginning with your feet and working up through your body, as described in Chapter 4. This is necessary because no matter how relaxed you thought you were before you began this process, you will be surprised at how much tension still remains in your body.

- Bring the light through, as described earlier, to cleanse away any remaining emotions of your own.

- Now take your mind to the lower part of your body, at the base of your spine and between your hips.

- Open your centers, but while doing so, draw your friend into your aura and up to the area of the second center, which is the abdominal area.

- Visualize the glass tube as before, and watch the smoke-like substance rising through the tube; then reach out to draw your friend into your aura again, and take both her energy and yours up to the third center, which is the diaphragm area.

- If you can, note any feelings you experience as you do this, but don't think about them too hard.

- Lastly, draw your friend into your aura and up to the fourth center, which is the heart chakra.

- By now, you should feel as though you have expanded several feet and grown taller.

When you have completed this process, quickly run through the process several times more to make sure you are totally ready.

Describe whatever pictures you can see in your mind to your friend. Explain how you are feeling, and give your friend time to respond.

If you can, try to extend your mind across to your friend each time your friend speaks, and bring her aura back into your centers, making your energy stronger. (Don't worry if you can't do

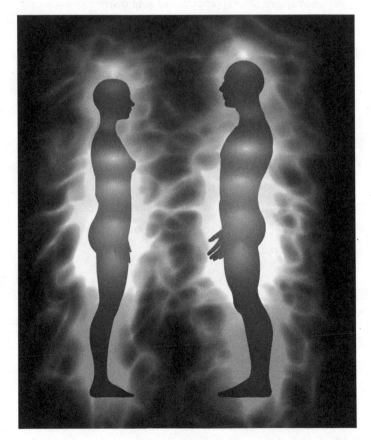

this at first.) It is important to say everything you see and feel, no matter how silly it may sound to you. Until you can learn to let go of yourself and drift along with the flow, nothing else will be able to come into your mind.

Auric reading can give you information only about the past and the present, so even if your friend cannot make a connection with what you have said, don't suggest that the event you are reporting has yet to happen. Move on to something else. No matter how close you and your friend are, there will always be things you don't know about your friend; whatever comes into your mind, though, do mention it, and then let it go.

After a while, you will feel yourself straining to see something, and each time you speak, the energy will decrease a little. Stir up the energy again, draw in your friend's aura, and bring it through your body to your heart center again. After about half an hour to an hour, you will feel depleted, so you should stop the session and close your centers.

With your mind, make sure you see the smokelike substance receding from the fourth center to the third center. Either push it down with your mind, or imagine a door slamming shut in this area. Continue by closing the third and second centers until the energy is once again settled at the base of your spine. Do not close off this center. As you close your psychic centers, you will feel yourself becoming smaller and more settled.

Finally, try to visualize yourself switching on a white light above your head. See the light flooding your whole body, running through your arms and legs and into the floor. Alternatively, imagine yourself standing beneath a waterfall, and feel the water running through your arms and feet and into the ground. Either visualization will have the same effect of cleansing anything you may still have in your aura from your friend, and grounding you again in the physical world.

• • •

Although this process will seem complicated at first, it will not take long to get the hang of it, and you will soon be able to do the exercise much faster. I advise that you try this only two or three times a week to begin with, because you will feel tired and depleted of energy if you do it more often. It is important always to relax properly beforehand, and make sure you open each center thoroughly before you start. If you work with your psychic centers in this way, mistakes are unlikely to happen, as you will be in control of what you are doing. Closing and cleansing should be a habit you get into, no matter where you are or what you are doing, as this will save you unnecessary psychic feelings or feelings of "invasion."

Cleansing with Light

If you ever feel tired for no reason, visualize the light or water coming down through the top of your head and out through your feet. Do this several times. Remember to do this after you've been shopping, for example. People drain you of energy, especially if you are in a crowd. By the time you get to the end of your shopping trip, you often feel like a limp rag! So remember to use the light or water to cleanse and ground yourself again. It will certainly help.

Two Clever Tricks

The aura is notoriously hard to see and to read, so you may end up leaving this and concentrating on easier forms of psychic endeavor, but here are two tricks that will at least allow you to get some kind of grip on this aura situation.

First, forget about seeing anything and focus on feeling the aura. Ask a friend to sit down and relax, and then ask her to sit with her feet forward so that you can reach them easily. Then ask your friend to close her eyes and just relax. Meanwhile, open your chakras quickly. Then squat down in front of her and start to pass your hands over your friend's feet at a distance of two or three inches, as though you were smoothing the air above the feet and ankles. Take your time over this. After a few moments, you will feel tingling or a slight resistance as you rub over the aura, and so will your friend. Once you have established that you can feel the aura, ask your friend to stand up with her back to you. Then pass your hands over your friend's back several times. Now, not only will you feel the aura and your friend feel you feeling the aura, but your friend will also start to tilt and then to almost fall backward toward you as the aura pulls her back.

The second trick is to place a friend on a chair by a plain wall. Look at your friend's head and upper body for a while and then close your eyes. If nothing happens, open your eyes again for a few moments and then close them again. This time, you will see the outline of your friend's head and shoulders come into view, surrounded by swirling colors.

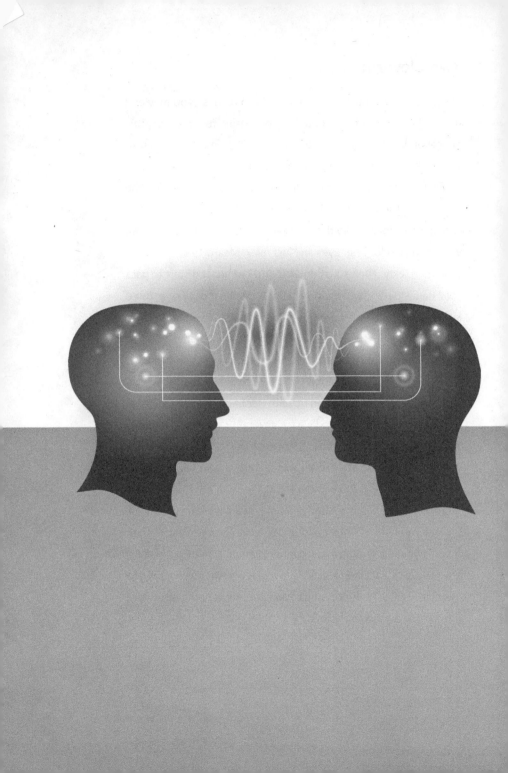

Different
Pathways

7

In the early days of developing your emotional centers, you will probably want to experiment with different methods of stimulating your psychic ability. There are so many pathways that you can feel overwhelmed by the choices available.

When I began my development, I looked at some of these different methods but allowed my intuition to guide me to what I felt would be the most interesting and appropriate choice to help me in my mediumship. I studied many books on different subjects, including tarot cards, playing cards, crystals, crystal balls, color, pendulum dowsing, and astrology, to name but a few. I met many people along the way who proclaimed loudly that their path was the best, but I found that I had no urge to go down many of these routes. You must also follow your own instincts.

In my childhood I had a strong interest in crystals. I had an old tin box in which I kept polished stones. Most were semiprecious stones that came out of brooches or pendants. I loved to hold them up to the sun and see the colors swirling in them. I suppose I subconsciously connected the colors with the auric ones I saw around people, animals, and plants.

When, as an adult, I saw that people were using unpolished crystals for healing, I felt sure that would be an important pathway for me too. Crystals have a living energy, and unpolished stones give off more of this energy than polished ones. So where healing was concerned, it made sense to me: combine the energy of the crystal with the energy of the psychic centers, and they must surely help the healing process. I soon found out, though, that healing in this way wasn't for me. I realized that it was the colors from the crystals that were drawing me in.

Somewhere inside me I still harbored that childhood link with color. It was then that I decided to study the effect that color has on the physical body, the psychic centers, and everything surrounding us. Like many people involved in New Age work, though, I still kept a number of crystals dotted around my home. I tried scrying with a crystal ball, but once again, it was the crystal that attracted me. Once I developed my mediumship, I found I didn't need to peer into the crystal to get clairvoyance, because I could already achieve this with my mind.

Divining with a pendulum was something I did become interested in because it worked for me. I have always kept one beside me in case I need a quick answer to something—and yes, it's made from crystal. When I work as a medium, though, I don't use any tools.

Despite my dismissal of many of these avenues, I have to stress that they work for other people, as we are all unique in our psychic abilities. What works well for one person will not work in the same way for anyone else. So my point is this: if you look at all the different areas that will help you to develop your psychic ability, do not think you have to emulate someone else, because what that person does may not be right for you. Always follow your feelings. You will know what your subconscious is telling you when the time is right for you to try something new.

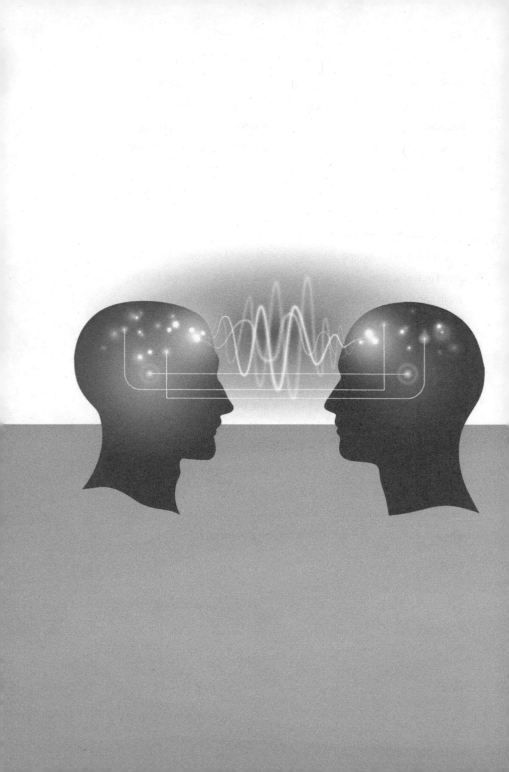

Tarot
as a Psychic
Pathway

8

One pathway I have incorporated to run alongside my mediumship is the tarot. I have always found the cards to be a brilliant tool for giving readings on a psychic level, especially if, for some reason, mediumship isn't possible. Ideally, to learn tarot you should take lessons or attend a workshop. You can teach yourself from books, and there are several accessible, easy-to-use titles that you can find in most bookstores. These seventy-eight cards are divided into the major arcana (twenty-two cards) and the minor arcana (fifty-six cards).

The major arcana cards represent the twenty-two universal principles or laws that we experience in different aspects and at different times of life. Jung called these principles major archetypes, or the kind of universal experiences that are understood the world over, regardless of cultural or family imprinting. So these twenty-two cards deal with twenty-two ways in which we grow, deepen, and evolve.

The fifty-six minor arcana cards are divided into four suits: swords, wands, cups, and pentacles. Some decks use different names for the suits, for example:

Wands:	Staves, sticks
Cups:	Chalices
Pentacles:	Coins, disks
Swords:	Daggers

These four suits show us the different energies that are used in the way we grow. For example, swords always indicate activity on a mental level, wands are symbols for intuitive and spiritual

aspects, cups reveal the emotional level, and disks reveal external reality, such as health, finances, relationships, and career.

I believe I was drawn to studying the tarot because it has a close link with astrology. As with astrology, a tarot reading can become very personal, and as with all mediumship, the psychic will have a strong desire to help, guide, and heal the person he or she is reading for.

If you are interested in developing your emotional centers this way, you first need to buy a deck of tarot cards at a New Age retailer where decks are available for review before purchase. You can also look on the Internet. Always take your time choosing. If you find yourself being drawn again and again to a certain pack of cards, then that is the one for you. Once you have opened the cards, never let anyone else use them because they will leave their own vibrations on the cards, and this may interfere in some way with your readings. Some tarot readers allow their cards to be shuffled by their clients, but others will not let anyone else touch their cards.

Each pack includes a small booklet that you can refer to, or you can buy a book that is relevant to the pack you are using. If you feel you need more information, there are many published books on this subject that you can choose from.

I taught myself to read the tarot, and although it took me quite a long time to learn, I found it very enjoyable. Always open your emotional psychic centers first, as described earlier.

Start with the major arcana, beginning with the first card, learning all the words that go with it, before going on to the second card. Study the picture on the card as well as the related words. See if you feel anything from the picture. Your feelings may not correspond with the words, but they will be right for you to use in your readings, so write these feelings down.

From the moment you begin using the tarot, your psychic ability will develop. When you practice or when you give a reading,
don't hold back; say anything that comes to you, because very
often your feelings will be correct.

Once you have studied the major arcana, try laying a small,
basic spread. You can find spreads in the booklet that came with
your cards or in any book on the tarot. I found I had so many vol-
unteers to practice on with the tarot, psychometry, and mediumship that people were contacting me at all hours for readings! If
you want to make your reading more detailed, you need to learn
the minor arcana too, so that you get a complete overall picture.

When I give a reading, I often combine mediumship and tarot.
First, I focus on the mediumship, because people often want to
know if their friends or relatives still live on after they have physically died. The spirits who make contact then try to give proof of
their survival. I follow this with a tarot reading, so that my sitter
has a complete overall picture of what life holds; the tarot reading often confirms much of the information that the client's spirit
friends have given.

It is frequently said that you cannot lay tarot cards for yourself,
but I have found this to be untrue. It is possible to get a reading
for yourself, but it is more difficult to do, because the cards will
indicate things you already know about. There are times, though,
when they give an answer that's different from the one you were
expecting. It is important that you don't run your life by consulting
the cards for yourself at all hours of the day and night, though. They
can become a bit addictive, so you should put them aside and con-
sult them only now and then, when you feel you have a problem.

The only time I have ever altered a reading was because I couldn't bring myself to tell the total truth that I could see in the cards. A regular client came over from Germany to see me for a consultation. When I saw her I barely recognized her, as she had lost so much weight, and her eyes appeared haunted. When I laid the cards for her, I could see that she had a serious illness, which was most likely terminal. I thought quickly and decided to tell her this information had to do not with her but with someone around her. She looked frightened, unsure of whether I was telling her the truth, and asked me outright if she was the one who was going to die. Again I told her it wasn't. Her look of relief told me I had given her the right answer. She died of cancer within a few months.

I know I was ethically wrong to lie, but I couldn't bear to add to her pain by telling her the truth. She would have realized before her death what I had done. Whether she thought of me then as someone who was protecting her or whether she thought I was a rotten tarot reader didn't matter. I did what I did for what I thought were the right reasons, to give her some form of hope for a little longer. Other people who give readings tell me that they would have done exactly the same thing in the same circumstances.

Normally, it's best to tell clients what you see for them, as long as you can do it in a gentle and helpful manner, but if you truly feel that your client is likely to die, keep the information to yourself.

Tarot cards are always drawn to the nearest emotional event in a person's life, so if someone is unhappy due to his or her relationship situation, this is what the cards will focus on. If you are reading for someone who is struggling with a business or financial matter, the cards will point you in that direction. The same goes for health, family matters, a desire to move, or anything else that is in the heart and mind of your client. Sometimes the nearest emotional "biggie" has happened a couple of years back. In this case, the reading will tell you (and the client) exactly what happened at that time, but it may not want to talk about the things that are going on in the client's life right now or move into the future. There is a way around this frustrating problem, and this is where you can start to hone your psychic channeling talents.

Pick the cards up and start shuffling them slowly. While you are doing this, silently ask your spirit guides to give you the information that the client wants to hear relating to the present and the future, as opposed to what was happening a couple of years back.

You can also use this technique if the cards harp on about one part of a client's life and don't want to move on and talk about other areas of his or her life. For example, they may go on and on about love but not mention finances, health, or the client's career.

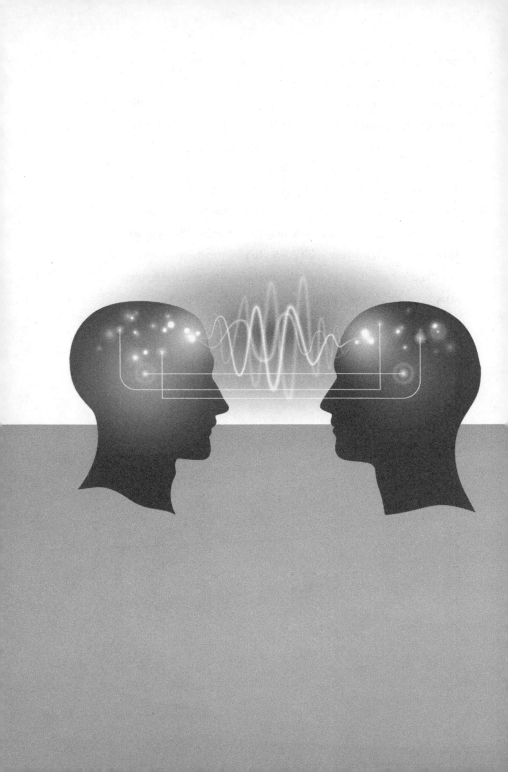

Psychometry

9

Psychometry is similar to auric reading, but instead of being person-to-person, psychometry is person-to-obect. In psychometry, the medium holds an object. The object can be almost anything, but it is usually a piece of jewelry.

For a psychometric reading to be effective, the psychometrist must hold the object in his or her hand while exploring it psychically. Everything in the physical world has its own aura, and an experienced psychometrist can easily read the emanations flowing from these items. Psychometry is supposed to tell you the history of the object itself, but nobody wants to have a conversation with a watch about its works, or listen to a pendant while it complains about the state of the chain that it hangs from. Of course, the psychometrist uses his or her skill to pick up information about the person who wears the item, and it is during the reading that the owner's personal life and personal problems become evident to the psychometrist

The object must have been worn only by the inquirer, because if another person wore it before the current owner, the psychic may well pick up feelings from that person instead, or a mixture of both. The thoughts and feelings of the previous owner may be stronger, thus overshadowing those of the second owner. (This is a little like dark paint showing through a lighter color.) If this happens, the psychometrist should make an effort to find out about the former owner in order to confirm the accuracy of his or her reading for the current owner.

Once this psychic faculty is developed, it can be extremely accurate as a guide to the lifestyle and feelings of an object's owner. Other mediums have had outstanding success with this method, finding psychometry an invaluable tool in their work with, among others, the police when looking for missing persons.

Psychometric Readings

If you wish to try this method, you should enlist the help of a friend. Ask your friend to bring you an article, the history of which he or she knows about. If the article is not personal to your friend, make sure that it is not handled too much or it will be contaminated by your friend's own feelings. Instead, it should be placed in a paper bag or envelope and left wrapped on a table until you are ready to work with it.

Before you handle the article, give your friend a pen and paper to jot down what you say.

- Wash your hands and wrists thoroughly under running water to remove any other emanations from your skin.

- Dry your hands with a clean towel or paper towel.

- As you would do with other psychic methods, sit down and unwind. Try not to think about what you are doing.

- Note the way you are feeling. Are you hot, cold, or nervous? Be aware of any feelings that you have because you can then distinguish any feelings that you pick up later that are not your own.

- Now relax thoroughly in the same way as you would for an auric reading. Open your centers, starting with the first center. See your energy again as a smokelike substance.

- With your mind, bring the energy up from the first center to the second center.

Do not extend your mind out to your friend, because you do not want your auras to mingle during this type of reading.

- Go back to the base of your spine and bring the energy up through the second center (at your abdomen) to the third center (in your diaphragm area).

- Take your mind back down to the base of your spine and bring this smokelike substance up again through the second and third centers to the fourth center, which is in your chest area.

- Repeat this process several times, gently running the energy straight through from the first (base) center to the fourth (heart) center.

Now you are ready to begin the psychometric reading.

- Remove the article from its wrapping and hold it gently in the palms of both hands.

- Once more, take your energy from the base of your spine up to your heart.

- Swing your mind out to the article, extending it in a loop like the shape of a capital D, and bring the energy back into your own aura.

The vibrations received during a psychometric reading are fast, so you must say immediately how you are feeling and what you are seeing from the moment you touch the article. Are you feeling different from before you started?

Has the article become hot? Does it vibrate? Have you got pins and needles in your hands? Can you see a color, a person, or a house?

Every time you speak, the scene and feelings will change. State what you feel. Never add to it. If you feel nauseous, say that you feel nauseous; don't say, "You've been sick," as you will undoubtedly be wrong. Each time you speak, you should extend your mind out to the article and bring the energy back into your own aura.

This process will seem quite slow at first, but with practice you will become quicker and you will find it easier to do. You will know when you've had enough, as your energy will fade and you will feel as though you're struggling. When this happens, place the object back in its wrapping, and wash your wrists and hands again under running water. Use the closing procedure for your centers and the cleansing procedure for your aura, to avoid keeping any negative feelings you may have transferred from the article to yourself.

If you are successful, you may have the makings of a very good psychometrist. However, it is vital to always remember to pass on exactly what you see and feel and never to add anything of your own.

If you are unsure of what you are experiencing, then say so, because the emotional centers do not have the clarity of the higher levels of spiritual communication. You should always be honest. When you take note of what you feel when using psychometry, you will be surprised at what you can achieve.

Flower Clairsentience

Flower clairsentience is another form of psychometry, but the emanations from a flower are much faster than those given off by an inanimate object.

A good psychometrist will be able to see and feel the birth of the flower itself, feeling the sun, rain, and earth, and the activity and movement of insects. Even the negative sensation of being pulled or cut can tug at the solar plexus. However, the majority of people who bring a flower usually want it read on a personal level, and this form of psychometry will reveal the higher aspects of the person who has held the flower.

The heart center is more active than usual here, working on the spiritual needs of the individual rather than the physical and material conditions. Holding a flower can help the medium trace important events in a person's life, and this can also show the amount of spiritual growth that the client has attained.

Your Own Flower Readings

Try reading flowers with the help of a friend. Ask your friend to bring you a flower instead of an object. Tell your friend to keep the flower in a water jar, or wrapped in a white paper towel, with a folded piece of wet paper towel at the bottom; the point is to keep the stem of the flower wet to prevent it from dying too soon.

As you've done for psychometric readings, hold your hands under running water and then dry them with a paper towel.

Sit, relax, and open your emotional centers. Unwrap the flower, or remove it from the water jar, and hold it gently in your hands.

Extend your mind out to the flower in a capital D formation and draw the energy back into your own aura.

This psychic method is much faster than psychometry using an object, so be ready for what you feel, see, or hear. If your friend doesn't understand the information you are giving, that's okay; just say what you are feeling, and then go on to the next thing that you feel. Unless you let go of what you are feeling, a kind of blockage occurs that prevents the next stage from happening. Your friend can always check on the things that you said by referring later to any notes that he or she made.

At the end of the session, once again rinse your hands, close your centers, and bring through the light or the water to cleanse and ground yourself.

Flower clairsentience can show a person's hidden mediumistic abilities, or even a person's more conventional religious pathway. When asking people to bring a flower for a reading, I have found they often choose one suited to their own spiritual vibrations, even though they are not consciously aware of this.

In one class, I asked each student to bring a flower and to place it on a table without my seeing it. When I began to psychometrize the flowers, I found that a small purple violet gave off the highest spiritual qualities. It further revealed that one of the men had brought it in. His personality came across as practical and no-nonsense, but inside, he was clearly harboring a compassionate spirit. He went on to develop into a first-class medium and teacher.

ball, and then the mist should clear. You may see symbols or pictures, and you should make a note of these to look over later. Scry only for half an hour to begin with. This is very important. A little scrying every day or every other day will be far more beneficial to you than long, infrequent sessions, because your body and mind will get used

to the mental discipline. When you have finished, close your centers and cleanse your aura with the light or water method.

After you feel you have accomplished this successfully, you can then work with someone else. As before, place your friend opposite yourself, and extend your energy out to him or her, drawing your friend's energy up through your centers. Tell your sitter exactly what you see and feel. When you begin to tire or struggle, close your centers, and cleanse your aura.

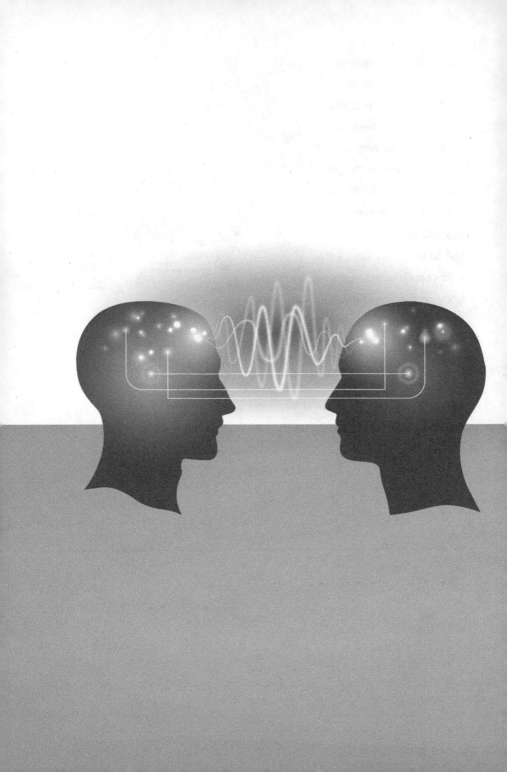

Astral
Travel

11

The third center, which lies in the region of the diaphragm, is the chakra that is responsible for creating the psychic phenomenon that we call astral travel, or out-of-body experience (OBE). As a child, I accepted astral travel as a natural part of my existence. I was a teenager when I discovered through my friends that other people did not do this, and it was only then that I consciously made an effort to prevent it from happening. I didn't want to be different from others at that time, and I didn't realize until later that many other people can, and do, travel this way.

The astral body is a replica of the physical body, but it is made of a much finer substance that is invisible to the naked eye. When the astral body is released from the physical body, it remains connected to the head of the body via a cord. This enables the astral body to stretch over long distances. The astral cord usually gives the appearance of being either silver or golden, although others have described it as a shimmering light. This cord disconnects from the physical body only at moment of death.

When I was young, I often myself out of my body, although I didn't explore very far, taking trips only around the house or garden. In the physical world, my parents would tell me not to stray too far or to speak to strangers, so maybe this advice and instinct prevented me from venturing outside those boundaries while in my astral form. At first, I would try to open doors, walk down stairs, and walk around corners. That's what I did while in the physical world, so the habit stayed with me for a while, even when traveling astrally. But it didn't take me too long to realize that I could walk or float through any kind of physical substance.

... easy to make ... get out of bed!

Overtiredness, illness, stress, or worry can bring on an OBE. It tends to happen when you are drifting off to sleep, when the state you are in is pleasant and comfortable, or when you are already asleep.

As a child, when I experienced astral travel, I would leave my body, meet my guides, and go to the world of spirit, where I learned about my future life. Later, as an adult, I returned and found someone asleep in my bed. This person was facing away from me, so I tried to push her out of my bed! I had no impact was s̶

caused me to slip back into the physical rea̶

happened on another occasion when I was an adult. I arrived back in the bedroom to see my husband lying beside a woman with his arm around her! Of course, I discovered that the "other" woman was me, and the surprise caused me to immediately align with my physical body.

There has been the odd occasion when I didn't enjoy the experience of astral travel. Once I woke up to find myself embedded in the middle of the mattress, among the springs and stuffing. I had turned onto my stomach while asleep, left my body, and gone downwar This happened during the paralyzing stage, because I woke up efore completing the detachment. On another occasion, I ha detached properly, but then shot up at a fair speed through e bedroom ceiling and into the attic. My journey took me thro gh spiderwebs and dust, and out through the roof. Althoug couldn't feel the spiders or their webs, my dislike and fear of ese little eight-legged creatures transmitted itself to my astral I dy, making me shoot down again and back into my physical se !

How to Experience Successful Astral Travel

This area of psychic exploration is fascinating, but there are several rules you have to abide by if you want to be safe and successful. It is important to prepare thoroughly beforehand, and the most significant aspect of this preparation is that you ensure that you are not disturbed in any way. Turn off the phone, and don't have any animals in the room with you. Try to experiment only if you are certain that no one will knock on your door or ring the doorbell.

- Go to your bedroom, which should be warm and dark. Once you are sure of peace and quiet, loosen your clothing and remove any items of jewelry.

- Sit on your bed, relax, and open your centers.

- Then stretch out and lie on your back.

- Take several deep breaths and go through the relaxation

routine, beginning with your feet. When you are fully relaxed, your mouth should drop open a little.

- Run the energy through your psychic centers once again, and if by this time you haven't fallen asleep, a few moments will pass until you find yourself entering a cataleptic state.

At this point, you may feel some apprehension, but try to let it wash over you. You may hear a sudden loud buzzing next to your ear. If this happens and makes you jump, try to relax again. You may be aware of a loud, rhythmic banging, but this is just the enhanced sound of your heartbeat. At this point you may be reluctant to take the process further. This is natural, but it will prevent your astral form from leaving your physical body. It is important to overcome this instinct, because each time you try, you will find it becomes easier to do. It is during the cataleptic stage that you may notice colors. Many mediums are aware of vivid colors before and during an OBE, so if this happens, you will know you are succeeding with your attempt at astral travel.

Stare at a point above your head, and tell yourself you are rising into the air, willing yourself to reach that point above your head. You may feel as though you are moving rapidly up and down, but this is the astral body attempting to free itself of the physical, and although it may seem difficult to do, try to allow it to happen without becoming agitated. All of this may seem like hard work, and there will be a few things to overcome before you are successful. Then again, you may not experience any of these things and everything will go quite smoothly. Once the astral body becomes free, it will feel more settled, and you may find yourself rising a few inches. At first this may not seem like much, but with practice, it will not be long before you are looking down on yourself from the ceiling.

If you become aware that your astral form is still in a horizontal position, just think yourself upright. Once again, it may take a little while to achieve this. You will need to be several feet away from your body before you are able to move around at will, so this will take some practice. When you want to return your astral body to your physical body, you must make sure you align yourself properly with your physical form. If you don't do this, you will have the uncomfortable awareness of being only half in, and this will make you feel irritable and unsure of what is going on around you. After you have returned to your physical body, lie quietly for a few moments. Close your centers before bringing the white light through the top of your head. Do this several times. Not only does this cleanse your astral body, it helps to realign it as well.

Once you have succeeded in these experiments, you should take note of your surroundings. Look at your physical self on the bed and then look down at your astral body, or look in a mirror. Check to see whether you can see the astral cord, which comes from the forehead on the physical body and attaches to the back of the head on the astral body. Even if the room is dark, the white light emanating from your astral self will glow slightly. If you look into a mirror, you will probably find that you have become younger looking. You will be back at the age when you looked your best, but often with an added beauty or glow.

When you feel able to take this process further, you will be able to walk through walls and closed doors, or pass through the ceiling. There are many instances of people who, while in their astral bodies, traveled thousands of miles to the other side of the world, or even into outer space. There are many recorded incidents regarding operations. Some people have watched themselves during a procedure and remember hearing the operating staff's conversations and seeing the instruments they were using. One friend who had perfected the art of leaving his body told me he would visit me at a certain time on one particular evening. Although I didn't see him, an invisible force knocked my lampshade violently and I felt an unseen figure rushing past me and out through the wall of my room.

Astral travel is a natural part of our existence. Even those people who say they have never experienced an OBE have traveled out of their bodies during sleep. It seems the physical body needs this to happen for the benefit of its health. Many ancient civilizations believed in astral bodies:

The Egyptians believed that each individual possessed an astral or spiritual second body in the form of a bird with a human face. At death, this astral body, called *ba*, departed the physical body but hovered close to it.

The Old Testament tells of the prophet Elisha, who flew through the air into the bedroom of a hostile Syrian king, where he eavesdropped on the king's military plans. Because of what he heard and saw, the Israelites thwarted a Syrian attack on their homeland.

Southern Africans who leave their farms and families to work in the gold or copper mines travel back in their astral bodies from time to time to check that their families are all right and to say hello!

There are many cave drawings, going back hundreds of years, of a replica body hovering above the physical, indicating that human beings have known about astral travel and a life after death throughout the centuries.

If you wish to take astral travel seriously, there are many avenues that you can explore. I cannot stress strongly enough that you should take as many precautions as possible to ensure you are not disturbed while attempting this practice. If you are, you will suddenly whip back into your physical body, which is a very distressing experience. Astral travel can be a very exciting area of discovery, but like physical exploration, it holds dangers for the unprotected. Always ask your spirit friends, relatives, or guides to watch over you while you are investigating the astral plane. You may even meet up with them on your journey. Never spend too long out of your body or stray far away, especially in the beginning. Remember, your physical body is lying in a cataleptic state on the bed, and if someone were to burst into your room, they might well think you had died!

If anything like this were to happen, you would still be able to return to your physical form, but you may feel unwell afterward because of the fright it has caused you. As long as you take precautions, however, you will find this a fascinating and rewarding experiment.

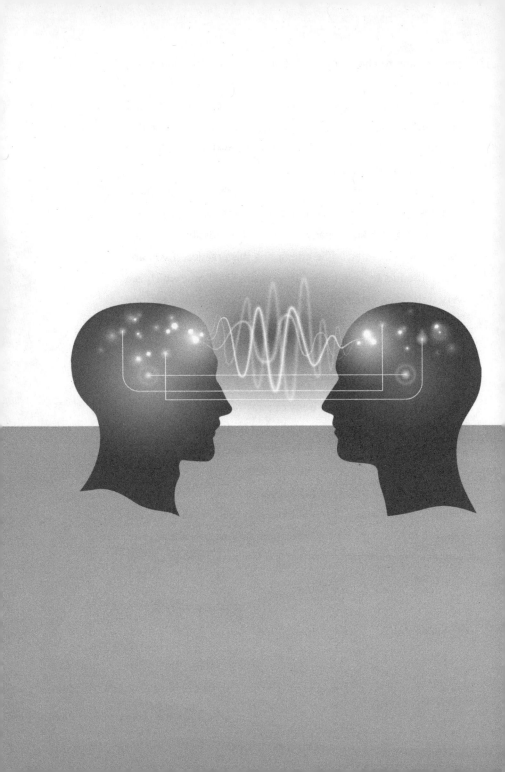

Psychic
Healing

12

You can give spiritual healing directly to a sick person or you can send that person "absent" healing from a distance. The fourth center lies in the region of the heart. It is this area that we use for healing. A kind of positive energy derives from this emotional center. It is the gateway to the faster mental centers that follow, and it works in conjunction with the fifth center, which is in the region of the throat.

Many people are natural healers without being aware of it. Sending out thoughts of compassion for another person will activate the fourth psychic center, allowing the positive energy to flow from the healer to the sick person. When we pray and ask God to make a loved one better, we are sending out our healing energy. When this does not work, we become dejected, often denying the very God we turned to in the first place.

There are various reasons why healing thoughts don't work. Sometimes a person is not responsive to healing because he or she has chosen to come to Earth in that particular incarnation

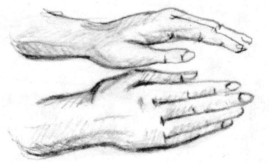

and to work through some form of karma that involves sickness at that time. Alternatively, it may be due to old age or because the body has gone too far to be healed. However, healing will always work on some level. If not physically, it will work on an emotional, psychological, or spiritual level, and it will make the sick person calmer and more able to cope with his or her problems.

Do you find that people are drawn to you, telling you of their troubles? Have you ever been on a bus or train that is almost empty, and yet someone comes to sit beside you and starts to talk to you? Afterward, do you often feel quite drained? If so, it is because the other person has depleted you of your natural healing energy. At other times, you might have noticed that you can pick up on the moods and temperaments of others, knowing instinctively, for instance, when someone is telling the truth or not. These are all aspects of the undeveloped healer.

Although you can gain quite a lot by working on your own in a healing capacity, you will achieve far more if you work in a class. In this way you will be able to develop your mental centers and build up a rapport with your spirit helpers, gaining far more from the knowledge they will impart than you could on your own. A qualification from a healing society will also open doors for you that are often closed to practicing healers without this benefit.

Some healers tend to dissociate themselves from trained mediumship, because they think that the energy they are using is different. However, healing power is psychic energy, and the natural healer can draw in this vitality before releasing it into the auric field of anyone who is in need. When working with a sick

person, the healer often feels the patient's pain and discomfort. This can help on a psychological level, because the patient feels that he or she and the healer are in tune with each other, and that the sick person can trust the healer implicitly. Healing energy comes from the emotional centers, and one can develop these centers to develop this psychic faculty, but if you also develop the fifth (throat) center, the added benefits are tremendous. With your fifth psychic center developed, as your guides draw close to you, they can direct you with their thoughts. Many times while I am healing, my guides give me further information, which is helpful to my patient and which gives me a clearer understanding of my patient's situation.

Conventional healing and spiritual healing should work side by side, although people often come for spiritual healing as a last resort, after having tried other methods without positive results. I always suggest that patients try healing once a week for six weeks, by which time they should have experienced some improvement. The success of this method does depend on the problem, though, as some problems are too deep-rooted to respond to psychic healing. Sometimes patients do not respond at all, or they don't give the healing process enough time to have a positive effect. Others expect miracles, despite the fact that they may have already tried everything else. In other cases, the positive changes begin immediately.

As soon as the healer touches the patient, energy is released. Once the session with the healer is over, the patient will feel very relaxed and will have a more positive outlook than he or she did before the session. The healing process should continue to have an effect throughout the days following the session, with the patient noticing small differences in any ailments he or she has. Sometimes the patient may feel worse immediately after the session but will improve quickly afterward. This effect is similar to taking prescribed medication for the first time. The physical body will not be used to the changes and has to adjust. In the same way, a patient may have to adjust to the healing energy working through the astral body and into the physical, although this doesn't take long to happen.

My brother has multiple sclerosis, which inhibits his ability to move around and live a normal life, so we arranged for me to give him contact healing. As we began the session and I touched his feet, I could feel powerful energy running out of my hands and up his legs. He could feel this phenomenon too, but the strong energy made him feel sick, so I stopped the healing. Because he felt so awful, he would not let me try again. I explained that the energy was stronger because of his serious condition, and that it should be less distressing at the next session. He still refused to have any more healing sessions, so I have resorted to sending out absent healing instead. This is a gentler method, but it can take longer to work.

Absent Healing

It is possible to send out absent healing at any time, but generally it is better if it's given at night, before the patient goes to sleep. The patient is often in bed or at least relaxed, and he or she will be more receptive at this time.

Before you begin, make sure you have a list at hand of the names of your patients and their ailments.

- Sit in a comfortable chair, relax, and open your centers from the base of your spine to your heart center.

- Bring the light or water through from the top of your head and out through your feet to wash away any emanations you may have in your own aura, because you don't want to pass anything on to your patients.

- It is important to ask your guides to draw close to you, and for you to know in your heart that they are there. Ask your healing guides to help you wherever possible before proceeding.

- Next, send out to your spiritual guides a mental picture of your patients along with their ailments. If you are unaware of what a patient looks like, concentrate on his or her name and problem.

- Wait a few moments, and then visualize your patients laughing and turning cartwheels, to show they are getting well.

- Afterward, thank your guides for their help; then close your centers and cleanse your aura.

It is more important than ever that you cleanse yourself after absent healing, because even with this indirect method, it is possible to pick up and retain a patient's condition.

You can follow the method described above for healing, or you can use another method that you feel more comfortable with. Some healers see their patients laughing and dancing around, and others visualize each person in a golden light. Whatever method you choose, it is always best to finish by seeing your patients happy and laughing.

Ask your patients to let you know each week how they are feeling, so you will know if the healing is working.

Contact Healing

If you wish to try contact healing, I suggest you choose a friend to work on first. Before your friend arrives, you should make sure that your body and your clothes are clean, and that you do not smell of strong perfume or cigarette smoke, which can be over-powering to the patient when in such close proximity to you.

- Wash your hands and wrists before relaxing and opening your centers, from the base of your spine to your heart center.

- Bring the light or the water through from the top of your head and out through your feet to wash away any unwanted emanations from your own aura, so that you do not pass these on to the patient.

- Your friend should sit sideways on a straight-backed chair that has no arms, so that it is easy for you to place your hands on his or her back. You should have a similar chair to sit on as you work.

- While you are standing, place your hands on either side of the patient's head.

- As you hold this position, ask your guides to draw close and to give your patient healing.

- Then stand or sit for the rest of the healing. Move your hands to the top of the spinal column and leave them there for a few moments.

- Then move them slowly down the back, stopping for a moment or two each time, until you arrive at the base of the spine.

- Concentrate on the link between your guides and yourself and on the energy that pours into your body and out

through your hands to the client. There is no need to put your hands on a specific part of the body, because the healing energy will automatically go where it's needed.

- Return your hands to the patient's head and mentally thank your guides.

- Close your centers and cleanse your aura.

While you are giving healing, you may feel warmth or heat coming from one or both of your hands. Your hands may tingle. If this happens, ask whether your patient felt anything. It is likely that your patient will have felt warmth from at least one of your hands. Some patients feel something even if you don't, so be sure to ask.

At the end of the healing the patient should be feeling relaxed, and you should advise that he or she take a rest in peace and quiet for an hour or two. Patients should definitely not rush around at this time.

• • •

Once you become more familiar with healing, you will be aware of subtle changes within your hands. One hand will be dominant, either becoming hotter or tingling more than the other, or you may be aware that one hand is drawn to a different area on the body from where you have placed it.

Because you are touching another person, and because your hands may be drawn, psychically, to other areas of your patient's body, it is always advisable for you to have another person in the room so that your client can't accuse you of touching him or her inappropriately.

Suggest that your patient make notes in the days that follow the healing session about anything that is relevant, and ask him or her to bring these notes to the next session. After your patient has left, wash your hands and wrists again.

Try this healing process for about four or five weeks to see whether you have any positive results. If you do, then you may wish to develop your healing ability further with a recognized healing body, through which you can develop to a higher level of mediumship.

It is important to remember that spirit is giving the healing rather than you. The spirits have chosen you to work with them because you have the type of energy necessary for healing to be successful. By ensuring that your own body is worthy of transmitting this energy, you will build up a wonderful rapport in your relationship with your spirit doctors and guides.

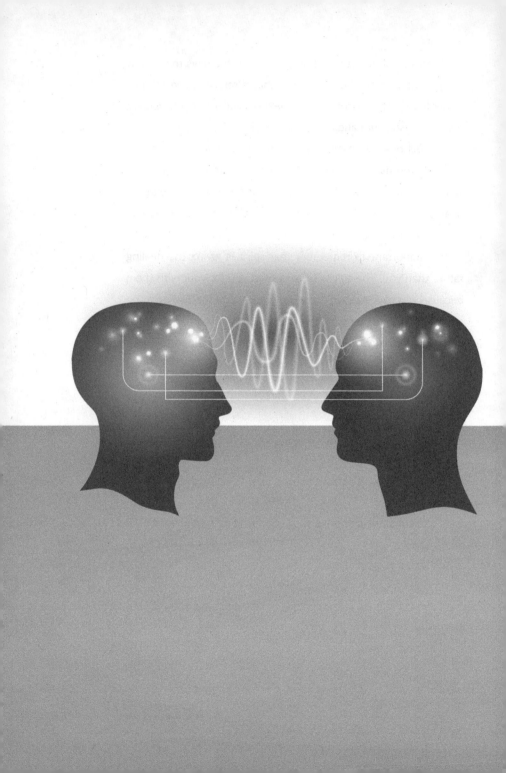

Mental Mediumship 13

The fifth center or chakra is the first of the mental centers. It is located in the area of the throat and deals with factual communication rather than feeling. There are two main categories that the fifth center deals with: objective and subjective.

Clairaudience

Clairaudience is the ability to hear a spirit guide or the voice of a person who has passed on to the other side. Sometimes this is a feeling of a voice in the head, but often it is almost real—as though someone were standing just behind you and whispering into your ear.

Objective Clairaudience

Objective clairaudience (or hearing spirit) is rare because it takes far more effort from the medium and spirits who do the communicating than subjective clairaudience does. The energy used is denser and requires some form of physical mediumship for it to happen. Despite this, most mediums have at one time or another experienced some form of objective clairaudience. I have heard voices and sounds outside of myself that have no physical explanation, always when I have least expected it.

One evening I was reading a book, with only my two dogs for company, and I heard my husband's car pull into our driveway. The headlights swept through the windows of the room, and both dogs jumped up to greet him. As the engine switched off, I looked out of the window to wave to him, but the driveway was empty. Surprised, I sat back down and picked up my book again. A

moment later, I heard the car again and saw the headlights flooding the room in the same way as before. This time it really was him.

Not only did I hear and see my husband's car before it actually arrived, but my dogs did too. I believe I was in a particularly receptive state at that moment because I was absorbed in my book. How many of us become engrossed in a book but are still conscious of sounds going on around us? These sounds do not normally disturb our reading despite the fact that we are physically aware of them. All animals are very receptive to psychic influences, so it isn't surprising that the two dogs lying at my feet would have shared this experience with me. What I heard and saw was loud and clear, but why I experienced this, moments before it actually happened, is still a mystery.

One hot summer's day when the air was very still, I was indoors with my eldest daughter, Karen. We were talking quietly when we both became aware of children laughing and calling to one another in our garden, along with the loud singing of birds. Both of us turned toward the open patio doors, but all the sound suddenly shut off and reverted to the silence that only a hot afternoon brings. It seems that despite the fact that we were chatting with each other, we were both in a receptive state, perhaps brought on by the heat and quiet of the day. Looking back on the incident, we are sure that what we heard was spirit children playing with one another, but as soon as we became aware of them, the clairaudience ended. These are only two examples of objective clairaudience, and both happened spontaneously.

I have experimented only once with planned objective clairaudience. I didn't really have much idea of what to do and was relying on instinct. After opening my centers, I asked spirit to speak to me through a tape recorder. I switched on the machine and sat quietly until the tape ended and the recorder clicked off. After rewinding the tape, I heard the words "My name is . . . ," but the rest was indistinct. The voice was deep, slow, and laborious and was accompanied by loud static. My husband, Peter, and I replayed the tape over and over again until we were sure of what was being transmitted, but we never made sense of the name. I didn't have the patience or the inclination to pursue this experiment, but there are many people who have obtained success in this way and who have received spirit messages by means of more sophisticated equipment.

Subjective Clairaudience

Subjective clairaudience is a voice heard in the head. It is similar to a thought, but it is very distinct from your own thoughts. It enters the mind from one side, usually close to the ear, and it returns to this area each time after communication. Normal thought fills the whole of the head and is there all the time. You cannot stop your thinking process, although it is possible to slow it down. When someone speaks to you by phone, you can still think while listening to what that person is saying, but his or her voice will be contained in one small space of your head and ear. Clairaudience works in a similar way. You are able to think, but while you are doing so, a small area opens up in your mind that is distinctly different in sound and feeling from your own thoughts. It is here that the voice of spirit makes contact through a special kind of link.

All spirit voices are different, and an experienced medium will recognize some of them. As with an ordinary phone line, there are times when the voices are difficult to hear, but a medium can ask the spirit to repeat the information until he or she is sure that it has been received correctly. Once the medium is sure of what spirit is saying, the message should be relayed exactly as it was heard, with nothing added. Many times I have received a message that made no sense to me—but it made sense to my sitter. If I had allowed my own feelings to enter into my readings, the information I gave my client would have been wrong.

Clairvoyance

Just as clairaudience provides sound that is beyond human range, clairvoyance (seeing spirit) produces vision in the same way. The sixth psychic center or chakra, the clairvoyant center, is the best known of all the psychic faculties; it is situated in the forehead between the eyebrows. It works almost simultaneously with the throat center, but the pictures a clairvoyant receives enter the opposite side of the head from the sound that is generated by clairaudience. Unlike the sounds received through clairaudience, the images received through clairvoyance spread throughout the whole of the mind.

Objective Clairvoyance

As with clairaudience, clairvoyance can be objective or subjective. Objective seeing produces solid visions that are indistinguishable from physical sight. For instance, on hearing Peter's car turn into our drive, I saw the sweep of headlights in our room, which is what made the whole experience so real.

Shortly after my father died, I spent a few days away with my daughter Nicky. We were sitting on the balcony of our hotel, eating breakfast and discussing our plans for the day, when both of us saw movement out of the corners of our eyes. Together, we turned toward the open doorway of our room and saw my father standing there. He appeared to be as solid as a physical person, even down to the shoes he was wearing. He was surrounded by a golden light and was smiling and holding out his hands. We both called to him, at which point he disappeared. Although we were amazed to see him, we realized that he had returned to show us that not only was he still alive in spirit, but he was also well again.

On another occasion I was working with my colleague Win Kent at the Spiritualist Association of Great Britain, in London. It was a late summer evening, and the night was drawing in. We had a full class, and the students were sitting in a meditative state, relaxed and with their eyes closed. We had placed candles around the room, and music was playing softly. Win was at the desk sorting through her notes to decide what she was going to do next, and I was walking among the students, checking that they were relaxed enough and ready for us to begin.

As I was walking around, I became aware of a light suffusing the room and looked up to see the most fantastic sight. Standing in front of everyone was the most exquisite angel. He must have been about seven feet in height, and he stood with his head bowed and his hands clasped in prayer. He was dressed in a long white gown that had silver bands at the neckline, hem, and sleeves. There was a large silver belt around his waist, and silver sandals on his feet. A narrow silver band was woven through his dark blond wavy hair. From his back grew two enormous wings that were so large that they were only inches from the floor. The feathers were brilliant white, with blue shadows between the folds. He was stunning. He stirred the most incredible spiritual emotions within me, and yet I could find no words to describe them.

I knew without doubt that I was in the presence of a celestial being of the highest order. The light emanating from him was flooding the room, and I stood still, watching him in wonder. I

briefly glanced around to see if anyone else had seen him, but the others still had their eyes closed. I didn't expect him to still be there when I looked back, but he was. With my eyes on him, I threaded my way across to Win and touched her, nodding in his direction. "Can you see what I'm seeing?" I whispered. She looked over to where I was pointing and whispered, "Oh, my God! He's so beautiful. He is an angel in the purest form." As we watched in silence, he slowly faded away.

The conditions have to be right for objective clairvoyance. The medium must be in a relaxed state, with centers open and a responsive mind. When my daughter and I saw my father, although we were chatting and eating, we were still relaxed and responsive, which allowed my father to show himself. Needless to say, the conditions in the class couldn't have been more perfect for the angel to materialize and to allow us to see him for several minutes. That experience was outstanding.

On yet another occasion, I was walking my dog around the perimeter of a recreational field, following a man with a black dog. The man was small in stature and appeared to be elderly, and he was wearing a gray raincoat and hat, although it was not cold or wet. As I walked along, I became lost in my own thoughts, but I was still aware that I was catching up to him. My own dog, an Irish Setter, had already run across the field. After a few moments, I realized that the man had disappeared. I looked around for him, but there was nobody else in the field apart from myself. I knew he couldn't have left the field because there was only one way in. He was walking too slowly to have gone far ahead of me, and I

would have known if he had turned around to walk back the way he had come. I could only conclude that, because of my contemplative mood, the man and dog were spirits.

Subjective Clairvoyance

With subjective clairvoyance, the medium can be more certain of what he or she is seeing. The medium can make these images larger or smaller, bring them closer so as to focus on one particular area, or "step back" for a wide-angle view. The effect is three-dimensional. It can be as though the medium is at the center of the picture, or suspended in the air and looking down on a scene.

I often "see" spirit standing between or behind people. This is "projected" subjective clairvoyance. The figures are not solid, because I can see through them, but they do have a semisolid quality about them. If I am with a group of people, I often see spirit figures walking among them. Some of them will place their arms around the shoulders of the people they have come to see, although those people will not be conscious of their presence. They don't always come around specifically for the purpose of asking me to give a message to their loved ones, but I am very aware that they are there.

One evening in my writing class, I became conscious of a spirit pushing between myself and another student. The spirit was so strong that the feeling that he was squeezing between us made me want to lean to one side to allow him room to get past me. I was trying to concentrate on the class, but he clearly wanted my attention, so I knew I had to describe him to my friend. I quickly scribbled down his description and the message that he passed to me—both of which turned out to be accurate, as the student recognized the description of the person and understood the message.

Unfortunately, clairvoyance needs clairaudience if it is to work properly. A medium can describe a spirit or a scene, but he or she also needs to hear why the person in spirit is showing the picture. With clairaudience, it is not necessary to have a picture to confirm a message, although any picture received usually supports the message. Out of the two vibrations, the receiver usually finds that one is slightly faster than the other. In my case, the clairaudience is faster. I usually hear a voice on the right-hand side of my head just before I see a picture, although they often seem to come together.

On a subjective level, spirit can show itself to more than one person at a time. I once asked my students to visualize a pen. Afterward, they all gave me a description of the pens they visualized, and naturally, each picture varied in some way. I then told them to open their centers, to ask spirit to show them a pen on a clairvoyant level, and to write down what they saw. Each student described exactly the same pen in precise detail!

To me, clairvoyance and clairaudience are the most important psychic faculties, because they represent true mediumship. Communication is a delicate process in which all the centers work together to produce a mixture of pictures and sensations. At times, I feel a glow or warmth, or even a sudden feeling of happiness. It may only be a sensation of "just knowing" that spirit is close. Development of the psychic faculties gives one the ability to know when this is the case.

Emotional mediumship can be extremely effective, especially in psychometry and healing, although healing can be enhanced through mental mediumship. To have the ability to see and speak to a person who has physically died is spiritually the highest level a medium can achieve, and if you think you have this ability, you owe it to yourself to develop it in the best way possible.

In my early days, I knew nothing whatsoever about spiritualism, or any aspect of the psychic field, apart from what was happening to me. Through trial and error, I eventually found my pathway, despite encountering many negative experiences during my journey. Even so, I have learned much from both positive and negative experiences, as they have enabled me to use them in my teaching. It is as necessary to be aware of the pitfalls as it is to teach about the higher aspects.

Conducting Your Own Mediumship

I strongly recommend that you sit with at least one other person to conduct your mediumship. There are many reasons for this. Safety is the first priority. When you open your higher centers, you become a beacon of light in the darkness on the lower astral plane. Any form of entity on this level will be drawn to your light. Heaven and Hell in their conventional forms do not exist in spirit, but there is a level to which those who have committed crimes are sent. It's a little like putting criminals in prison on our physical level. Once they have served their time and—hopefully—have learned to be better people in their future lives, they are freed.

Similar conditions exist on the astral plane. Criminals have to atone in some way before they can be brought back into the light of the higher astral plane. So if you are on your own, and you open all your centers without anyone to work on, you will build up a high level of energy without any form of release. Anything drawn to you can slip into your aura, and you will be left with the sensation of being half in and half out of your body, and at the same time you will be aware that another mind is in there with you!

This is one of the main reasons why there are developing circles and classes. A reputable class will have an experienced medium in charge, and this person will see exactly what is going on with everyone. A skilled medium can see the spirits who are with you, and how well you are working. Circles and classes also allow you to use your mediumship to work on other people.

If you feel you don't want to join a class or circle at this time, you will still need someone to practice on until you become experienced. Ask a friend to sit with you, preferably someone who has an open mind and who can remember friends or relatives who have passed into spirit. You must tell your friend, though, that you cannot guarantee anyone coming through; you can only ask spirit for contact—you cannot demand it.

- Ask your friend to sit on a chair opposite you and to relax as much as possible.

- You must then relax yourself thoroughly, and open your emotional centers as before.

- Now extend your energy in a capital D formation to draw your friend's energy into your aura.

- When you reach the throat center, you may feel a lump in your throat or even a small pain. You may feel slight pressure in one or both ears, or you may want to stretch your neck. The energy will be moving very quickly at this point.

- You should acknowledge what you are feeling, and then continue drawing up the energy and bringing your friend's into your own aura.

- When you lift the energy up to your forehead, between your eyebrows, you may experience a slight pain in this area. All of these sensations are signs that your centers are opening properly. If you don't feel anything, don't worry: you may have always been mediumistic and your centers may have naturally opened on a regular basis without you realizing it.

- By this time, you should feel very tall, as though you have expanded in all directions, and feel very light within yourself, almost as if you are floating.

- After you've opened the throat and eye centers, you should bring the energy right out through the top of your head. Gently run the energy through your centers, from the lowest chakra and out through your head.

- Do this several times without extending your mind out to your friend.

- Then you should ask your spirit friends to draw close in order to give both of you protection and to give communication to your friend.

After a few moments you will see the mist that you saw before while pulling energy up through the centers. There will be brilliant sparks of light flashing through this mist. It is important to stay relaxed, so if you feel yourself tensing up, make a conscious effort to relax, and gently run the energy up and down your own body again. After a few moments, the mist should clear and you will be aware of a brilliant golden light in the blackness behind your eyes. Look through your mind toward this light, not at it. It's like looking through the crystal ball and not at the surface, or ignoring rain on the windshield of your car and concentrating on the road ahead.

Sometimes it is possible to be looking at something while all the activity is going on behind it. If you continue, you should then be aware of a thought in your mind that you know isn't one of your own, or a picture that isn't a product of your own mind. You may well have both. The picture may not be of a spirit person—it can be of a street scene, for instance—but whatever you get you should immediately pass on to your friend to write down. Remember to relay the image exactly as you see it. Do not add anything.

Once you have given the information to your friend, you should draw the energy up to your clairvoyant eye again, extend your mind out to draw in your friend's energy, and once more immediately say what you see or hear. If you feel you are hearing only part of the message, bring the energy up to your throat center, and ask spirit to repeat the message until you feel you have heard it correctly. You can do the same with clairvoyance. You can ask the spirits to make the picture smaller or larger and they will do so. At first you may find that the picture is a bit fuzzy or dim, or that the message is a bit hit or miss. This will be because it is the first time spirit has worked with you in this way and you both need plenty of practice with each other before you can get it right.

Clairsentience

Clairsentience (sensing or feeling spirit) is a more common form of mediumship than clairaudience or clairvoyance. It is the ability to sense or feel things or spirit around you. You may be able to smell perfume or cigarette smoke, when you know there isn't any reason why you should. You may feel pressure from spirit, in the way that I did when spirit wanted to get past me while I was sitting in my writing class. You may feel a light touch on your head, neck, or arm. Once you have opened up your centers in the same way as for clairaudience and clairvoyance, you may feel spirit standing very close to you. You will have the urge to describe the entity through "feeling" or "sensing" the spirit's size, age, or other characteristics. You may have an overpowering urge to pass on a message even though you haven't heard a voice or had a thought. You may feel very hot or cold, happy or sad, bloated or thin, or even in pain from the way the spirit died.

These sensations are not the same as what you feel by opening your lower centers, and it is only when you reach this stage in your development that you will be able to tell the difference between the two.

I once had the spirit of a man who had committed suicide come through to me. He clairvoyantly showed me a picture of himself hanging from a rope in his garage, but I also had the impression of the rope around my neck, which was gradually becoming tighter and tighter. I had to ask him to stand back from me until the disconcerting sensation disappeared.

When you use all of your psychic centers, you will experience a mixture of all of their effects, but only with time and practice will you recognize this. Opening all your psychic centers and using them in this way will be very draining. Even experienced mediums work for only about an hour with one person before having to close their centers to rest for a short while. If you feel yourself beginning to strain, you should close your centers and bring through the light or the water to cleanse your aura. Always thank your guides, because even if you didn't see or hear anything, they will have been close by, watching over you.

To be successful, you will have to work like this on several occasions before you consider joining a group or class. In the beginning, you will think you are hearing messages from spirit, but in fact they will be auric in origin (that is, from the mind of the person you are reading) rather than from spirit.

The same may apply to your clairvoyance. It is only with practice, practice, and more practice that you will become proficient enough to work with the public. Therefore, if you feel that after a few attempts you were successful working with your friends, I urge you to join a class where you can work with several people. When you have a dozen or so people in a group, the energy is far stronger than with only one person, and success will come faster. After all, if you have truly worked toward this moment, you will want to attain the highest level that you can, and it is possible to do this only under the supervision of a professional medium.

When you sit with a group of other developing mediums, you will also discover the direction in which you will eventually be working. There are many pathways along which you can take your mediumship. Most mediums give private readings, but they also often work as platform mediums for Spiritualist churches, relaying messages for audience members to dead relatives whom they want to contact. Others develop as psychic artists, aura color readers, or spiritual healers. Only in a circle can the presiding medium tell you if you have trance potential or if you are a physical medium. There are many directions in which you can take your mediumship, and you will find that spirit will guide you in the direction that is right for you.

We are all unique, and each medium will be able to do something that another medium can't. For instance, apart from giving sittings in the usual way, with someone in front of me, I can also use a letter to make contact with spirit. If someone needs a reading but I cannot fit him or her into my schedule for a period of time, I will ask that person to send me a handwritten letter for me to tune in to. I ask the person not to put actual questions in the letter but to scribble over the page or write some nonsense. I then tune in to his or her aura by holding the letter. This is not psychometry, but a link from my sitter, through me, to spirit.

In this way, I can do the reading at any time that I want—before I go to bed or, if I prefer, in the early hours of the morning. The other advantage is that I can go on to the highest level within myself and relate whatever I see or feel by recording what I receive on a cassette tape, without any interruptions from my sitter. I'm not saying that your sitter shouldn't interrupt you—far from it. The sitter often needs to clarify a point, but each time that the sitter speaks to you, your energy drops. If a question has been asked, then that is always in your own mind too. By working in this way, I stay on that higher level throughout the reading. I always record my readings, and I ask my sitters not to throw the recording away, but to keep it safe and play it now and again. A certain point that perhaps they didn't understand on the first reading will usually become clear after a period of time.

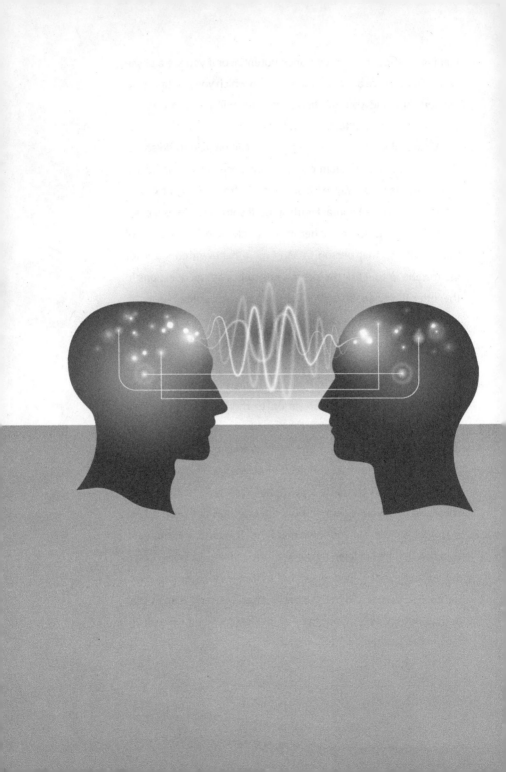

Fate

I never believed in fate until I developed as a medium, but so many things that have happened since have convinced me that fate had marked me out to be a medium long before I was aware of the fact. Many mediums say they don't predict the future, but spirit will often give guidance for future events, along with messages to loved ones.

For example, this is what happened when one of my regular clients came to see me. This client always wrote down everything I received during the reading so she could check it out when she had the chance. On this particular occasion, spirit told me that her son was working abroad, and that he was thinking of divorcing his wife.

"No, that's not right," she said. "I know they are both very happy. I only spoke to them a few days ago."

I went back to spirit to check that I had heard correctly. "My guide is telling me again that your son is not happy and that he will divorce his wife," I repeated.

"I'll write it down, although I know it isn't necessary because it just isn't true." She was defensive.

Spirit then showed me a picture of a woman who was on the earth (still alive), and I described the woman to my sitter and asked if she recognized her. I also gave her the name Kim. (I have changed the name here, for reasons of privacy.)

"No, I don't recognize the woman or the name," she said.

"Well, I can only give you what I'm being told or shown, and my guide says that your son will marry this woman."

My sitter was so amazed that she shook her head several times and then laughed. "I will phone him when I get home to tell him what you said."

Because of her disbelief, I didn't think I would hear from her again, but two years later she phoned for another appointment. She also asked if she could bring someone with her. Of course I said it was okay. When she and her companion came to see me, I looked at the younger woman with her and said, "I know you. Have you been to see me before?"

"No, never."

"Well, I must have seen you somewhere," I said, "because your face is very familiar." At this point they both burst out laughing.

My sitter said, "I had to come to you today to tell you how right you were about my son. You said at our last sitting, two years ago, that he would get a divorce and remarry."

She handed me a piece of folded paper, yellowing slightly with age. "I wrote everything down, although I didn't believe a word you said. You gave me the description and name of the woman that he would get married to. I phoned him after I left your house, and he told me that it was such a lot of rubbish because he and his wife were very happy. But a year on, his marriage folded and he did divorce his wife. A few months afterward he met the Kim you told me about. And this is she."

No wonder I thought I knew Kim from somewhere. There wasn't any way that the son knew he would meet Kim. It was a long time after his mother's reading that his marriage fell apart and he divorced his wife, and even more time elapsed before he met Kim.

It was impossible to make something like this happen, but it had happened exactly as spirit predicted, and his mother still had the piece of paper on which she had written it all down.

This is only one incident that helped to change my view regarding fate and the fact that our lives are mapped out for us before we are born. Here is another, more serious one.

Peter's Son

One day during a meditation I had been taken to the spirit plane and into the Temple of Life. (This is a beautiful building that I visit when spirit needs to show or teach me something.) In my meditation, I walked up the wide marble steps and into a huge room where there were two lecterns placed on opposite sides of the room. Standing in front of one was a friend of mine with whom I had lost contact over the years. I was shocked to see him in spirit because he would still have been young had he lived. He was dressed in white robes, which also surprised me, for this indicated that he was working as a guide of some kind. When he was alive, we never spoke to each other about psychic things.

He called me over to the lectern next to him. There was a huge book standing open on it, and he pointed halfway down a page. The name "Caulfield"—my and my husband's surname—stood out, and I asked him what it meant.

"This is the Book of Life," he said. "When someone in your world dies, the name is entered into this book." He then pointed behind him at several long glass cases that appeared to be similar to coffins.

"These are a few of the people who have come to us after their death." He turned and pointed across the room. "Over there, my colleague is writing in the names of those about to be born into your world."

I turned and looked. There were several more glass coffins spread around. We walked across, and the other spirit guide gave me a smile and continued writing in his book. When I looked into the coffins, I saw people of all races, ages, and genders.

"You are surprised that there is a mixture of adults and children waiting to be reborn." My friend smiled at me. "This is because they are incarnating and have done so several times before. The younger they are, the newer they are to this, but when they reach your physical plane, they all begin again as a baby."

Shortly after this, the guide indicated that I should come out of my meditation and return to real life. I told Peter of my experience, and we both had the thought that perhaps one of us was going to die. We tried to push it to the back of our minds, though.

A few months later, just before Christmas, we invited two friends to stay with us for the holiday. One day, although we had the central heating on, we decided to light a log fire to make the place more Christmassy and cheerful. We were all sitting around the table finishing lunch, when Peter got up to put another log on the fire. He called out to us to come over and look. In the grate was a burned-down log that was gray with ash. Within the ash was a moving picture of Peter's face, showing him crying and contorted in pain. We were transfixed with shock. Both of our friends were mediums, and we explained what I had seen during my meditation.

At this point we were really worried, knowing that whatever was going to happen was connected in some way to Peter. That evening we were watching television when our doorbell chimed. Peter got up to answer it, but there was no one there. We thought it must have been the wind, although it wasn't particularly windy outside. As he sat down, the bell chimed once more, but again, there wasn't anyone there. This time Peter swore under his breath and took the batteries out of the doorbell.

The following morning our friends left us to return home. We were puttering about doing one thing or another when the doorbell chimed yet again.

"How the hell can that happen?" Peter said. "It's impossible without the batteries."

"Perhaps there's a fault somewhere in the wiring."

We both knew we were clutching at straws, but Pete pulled out all the wiring, completely dismantling everything.

Despite this, the doorbell chimed intermittently during most of the day. By then we had both realized that it was probably spirit trying to tell us something, so I decided to tune in to find out what was going on, but no one came through to speak to me. That night we were both sound asleep when I was awakened by something. Suspended in the air over the bed was a round, red light. It was about the size of a large marble. As I gazed at it, Peter woke up too.

"What's that?" he asked.

"I don't know," I said. We watched for a few moments more and then fell asleep again.

A few weeks later, I was in the spare bedroom speaking on the phone when a painting fell off the wall. When I examined the back of the painting, I found no reason for this to have happened. I knew that a painting falling off a wall often predicted a death, and in fact that had happened a short while before my father died. So by this time we knew something unpleasant was heading our way, but I couldn't find out what it was because spirit wouldn't tell me.

Several months passed without further incident. Then, one early summer's morning I decided to have a bath. First I turned the answering machine on in case anyone phoned. I had almost finished drying myself when I heard the phone ring and the answering machine turn on. I dressed and then checked the machine to see who had called, but all I could hear was the swishing of my own dishwasher! Interestingly, the answering machine didn't pick up and record the sound. After I told Peter about this, we were both on edge, because by then other strange things were happening too, such as the television changing channels all the time.

Then one night in late summer our doorbell rang. This time when Peter answered the door, it was the police. They said that Peter's son was in the hospital in serious condition. When Peter went to visit him, he found out that his son, who had a serious head injury, wanted to discharge himself from the hospital against the wishes of the staff. Despite all attempts to get him to see sense, he left the hospital. Two days later, he collapsed and died.

Needless to say, Peter and his ex-wife and family were all dev-astated. I had been shown the surname Caulfield many months before by spirit in the Book of Life, but I hadn't for one moment thought it would be one of Peter's children. There had been many warnings, so after the funeral I asked spirit once again why it hadn't been possible to tell me.

"If you had known," spirit told me, "what would you have done? You could not have prevented it from happening. It would have been impossible. We could only prepare you for the worst."

I realized how right this was, but it also made me see again that our lives are worked out for us before we are born, and that our time of death is preordained.

My Daughter

A few years later, I was sitting alone meditating and found myself again outside the doors of the Temple of Life. This time the heavy oak doors were shut, and in front of them stood a guide with a long beard. He was dressed in black robes, and he held a long staff in each hand. His hands were crossed over each other at waist level. Pierced through each staff were five skulls. I asked him what the skulls meant, and he said he couldn't tell me. So I asked him if I could enter the temple. He told me, "No."

I left feeling puzzled, but after our previous experience I knew something serious was again going to happen. After that day, whenever I meditated and was taken to the temple, I saw the same guide with the skulls, standing in front of the door. I began to worry about this, so I tuned in to ask my own guides what was happening. They said they couldn't tell me either, but that it would all become clear in time. Whenever I tried to pursue my questioning, they stopped communicating or changed the subject.

About a year later, we went to Cornwall for a short holiday with two friends, and while in a gift shop, we came across a model of a man dressed in robes, holding a staff that was threaded through with a couple of skulls. This brought back the memory of my meditations, but I tried to put it out of my mind. A few months later, I began having dreams in which I could see ten skulls scattered in the earth and dust. The dreams were so vivid that I knew they were clairvoyant. I had the dreams on a monthly basis, but each time there would be one skull missing, and over a period of ten months they disappeared altogether.

Although the dreams had ceased, other weird things happened that couldn't be explained. On one occasion, I took my dog for a walk in the forest, along with a friend. Although I was carrying my cell phone, it was turned off, because I used it only in an emergency. On arriving home I saw the red light flashing on my landline answering machine. When I played the message back, I heard myself and my friend having part of the conversation we'd had while in the forest! For this to happen, I would have needed my cell phone to be on. I would then have had to dial my home number and leave the line open while we were walking around. My home number wasn't programmed into my cell, so there wasn't any way I could have accidentally dialed it. After hearing the message, of course I checked my cell phone again and found it was still off. I waited for the telephone bill to arrive to see if the call had been logged, but it hadn't. I then asked an engineer if it was possible for this to happen, and he said it couldn't. I still have that tape.

Almost three years after first seeing the skulls, I began to think that my fears were groundless, but then one morning my youngest daughter, Nicky, telephoned for a chat. During the conversation she said that she had some bruising over her legs and arms but couldn't remember hurting herself. I urged her to go to the doctor, saying that bruising was sometimes a symptom of a blood disorder, even of leukemia. She laughed, saying that I worried too much, and then I heard her doorbell ring in the background, and she said she had to go. The following day she phoned again to say that although she was feeling okay, she had taken my advice and gone to have a blood test.

My stomach was churning, and I had a terrible feeling about this. My worst fears were realized when two days later she was taken to the hospital, where it was discovered she had one of the most aggressive types of leukemia. She stayed in the hospital for a period of ten months, during which time she underwent several operations, and was put on life support three times. On several occasions we were told to prepare for her death, but she pulled through each time. Eventually, she went into remission and came out of the hospital, and I began to hope that she would be okay. But this awful, dreadful churning in my stomach wouldn't leave me. My lovely daughter had been home for only two weeks when she suddenly collapsed and died.

It was some time afterward when I realized I had been warned about this for the past three years. The ten skulls I had been seeing were the ten months left of her life. Both of our children were in their thirties when they died. Peter's son was still single, but my daughter was married with two small children. It was the most horrendous time in both of our lives and the only time that I have wished I weren't mediumistic. But how would I have reacted if there had been no warning? The shock would have probably been much worse both for me and for the rest of my family. Somewhere, on some level, I was being prepared, although it didn't appear to be that way.

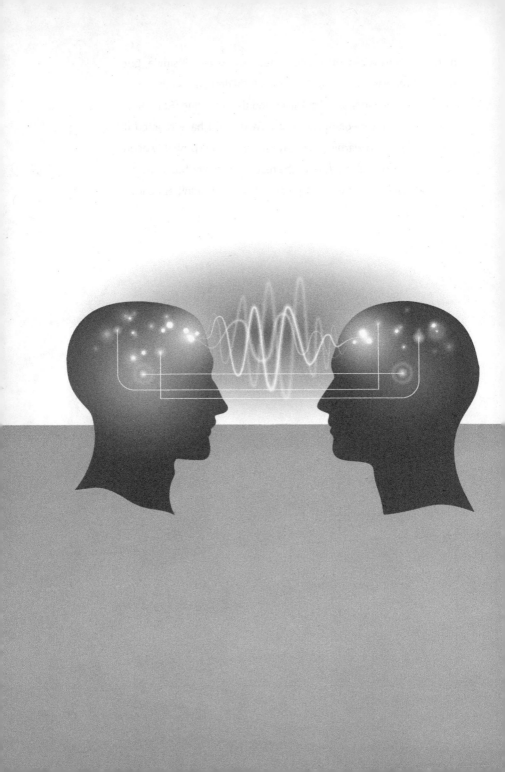

Preparation for Development as a Medium 15

Before experimenting on the highest psychic level or looking for a suitable class, it is important to consider the reasons *why* you wish to develop your psychic ability further. Developing as a medium is a serious decision, one that should not be taken lightly. Once you have taken your first steps on the pathway, you are undertaking a calling that will be with you for the rest of your life. It will be necessary to surrender completely to the influences of the spirit world, and to become a bridge between them and those who are seeking help and support. You must learn to forget about yourself in order to achieve the highest standard of mediumship possible, and this self-effacement is perhaps one of the hardest things of all to do.

If you want to become involved because you think it will help you to speak directly to relatives or friends who have passed over, then you should forget about development. Instead you should visit a reputable medium through whom spirit can contact you.

Mediumship requires a positive attitude. You may be full of doubts in the beginning because your psychic power works independently of your brain, and you have to assure your conscious mind continually that you are worthy. Spirit would not have chosen you if the spirits did not think you could do this. Doubt and confusion can inhibit psychic development. Your psychic energy is a reality, but learning to interpret it on a conscious level requires training. When you are at this point, all kinds of excuses prevail to prevent you from taking the next step. So dismiss your reservations and remain positive.

- Do you really believe you cannot die?

- Do you believe that you have come into this life to fulfill some specific purpose?

- Do you accept this experience as a means for spiritual growth?

At this point, you may wonder why you should consider these questions when you are interested only in developing your psychic energy. Any doubt about your own convictions will color your development and cause you to question your achievements, thus delaying your progress.

Before you pursue mediumship, you should speak to other mediums. Find out how they felt before their own development. Go to Spiritualist churches. Judge for yourself the quality of mediumship and see whether you think it is good or bad. Tell yourself you can do better. How could you possibly convince others of the power of spirit unless you are convinced? Having said all that, there is no doubt that if spirit wants you to be a medium, trying to wriggle out of it will not work. If God and your spirit friends want you, then they will find a way to make this clear to you—as I know only too well.

The next step is to learn your psychic mechanism thoroughly. Find out how your psychic power operates. This energy will activate on a finer and faster level of consciousness than your physical one. Communication registers via the psychic centers, which in turn transmit feeling and information to the brain. This shows the kind of mediumship that you are capable of and that is the most suitable for you.

Healing power operates on the emotional centers and will not work if the medium tries to develop only the throat center or clairvoyant eye. It would be like using a hair dryer to boil a kettle—the heat is there, but the purpose is different. Thoroughly developing the foundation before you attempt to exercise your mediumship will save you tremendous disappointment. When you discover the most accurate level for you to work on, you can concentrate on that direction.

I once knew of a mediumistic woman who had the ability to develop her healing, but she craved only to be clairvoyant. This longing prevented her from developing properly. She could have expanded her clairvoyance, which would have helped her tremendously with her healing, but she wanted to use it for giving messages. Spirit could see that her healing energy was the strongest, and that on any other level her mediumship would have been mediocre.

When spirit selects a person for mediumship, the person is directed toward a particular purpose. It is important to discover the right direction in the beginning of your process, and then to concentrate on being the best that you can be in the area that fits. Once you have considered everything and decided to go ahead, you should do so in the knowledge that you will play an important part in proving that we die only on a physical level. You can be that bridge from the spirit world to the physical.

Practical Matters

At this point, you need to work out several factors within your own mind and heart, and you must be completely honest with yourself before you decide on your future route. The woman who should have been a healer but who wanted to be a clairvoyant is not alone. It's likely that her motivation was a desire for excitement, a yearning for instant results, and an internal need to "feel clever." Giving readings or sittings can satisfy these desires, while, sadly, healing doesn't. Healing is undoubtedly extremely effective, but it works slowly and quietly, and it often requires several sessions for the effects to accumulate within the client's body and to work its magic. It is only in storybooks that a client leaps from a wheelchair, shouting that he or she can walk.

Sadly, no matter how many boring lectures the church president gives about "not allowing the ego get in the way," this effort must inevitably fail. Mediums and healers are justly proud of their gifts, while center committee members can be the worst offenders where officious behavior and "size of one's head" are concerned.

Only you can work out whether you want to progress from being someone who is vaguely interested in being a psychic, to being a one-of-many medium, to a much-in-demand top dog who can hold a church or theater audience spellbound. Only you can decide to climb the greasy pole of church and center politics.

Another decision that can come surprisingly early is whether you should work as an amateur or a professional. Amateurs frequently look down their noses at those who work for money, saying that they are using their "gifts" for personal gain. They should consider themselves lucky that they have sufficient income that they don't have to turn to their psychic gifts to sustain themselves and their families. It's worth bearing in mind that amateurs can get away with sloppy work, and they can refuse to do a job because they feel off color, they have a family crisis going on, or they don't like the client or the theater into which they have been booked. Professionals don't have these options. Professional psychics are worthy of our praise and encouragement.

Conclusion

Hopefully, you've discovered how easy it is to develop a modicum of psychic ability. After all, the psychic faculty is a natural part of our personality, and it is something that everyone has. If you become aware of it, you should trust it and use it for good purposes. However, you need to know how to listen to yourself first, and you can do that by devoting a few minutes of each day to meditation. If doing so simply isn't possible, one or two meditation sessions a week will still help you to enhance your psychic ability.

You would do well to explore the psychic field in bookshops and via the Internet, and at Spiritualist churches, psychic fairs, lectures, and demonstrations. As soon as you decide that you want answers, teachers and spiritual leaders will pop up and help you to find the answers. Psychic ability isn't mysterious, and it isn't just something for some chosen few; it is for everyone who wants to know about it. It reinforces your natural gifts, and it allows you to follow the path your gifts have laid before you.

Even if you do not wish to pursue your psychic gifts any further, I hope it has set you thinking. After all, there is more to life than science and logic, and although these are important and we shouldn't forget them, we need to keep a balance between them and all our other senses. I wish you good luck, love, and happiness in your search along your personal pathway.

About the Author

Ann Caulfield was born in Kingston-upon-Thames, Surrey, in England. Mediumistic from birth, she had childhood visions, out-of-body experiences, and she saw and spoke to spirit. She saw colors and lights around people, animals, and plants, and she believed everyone else saw these too. As a teenager she discovered that her friends did not share these same experiences, so, out of fear that they were not "normal," she tried to prevent them from happening. After being involved in a car crash, which she had previously dreamed about, she realized that she had to do something about the psychic energy that was taking over her life.

She was advised to seek help from The College of Psychic Studies in London, where she was invited to develop her psychic ability under the tutelage of Ivy Northage, one of Britain's leading mediums and teachers in psychic development. From the first lesson everything fell into place and Ann rapidly progressed. Ann went on to study the effect of color under the tutelage of Win Kent, a leading medium in her own special field of reading the colors of the aura.

Ann has worked as a professional medium, healer, and teacher of psychic development for almost forty years.

Other Titles in the *Plain & Simple* Series